Fast & Faster!

The Racing Stories of

"Chargin' Charlie Hayes"

Fast & Faster!

Contact:

Charlie Hayes

4195 West 7th St Apt 133

Reno, NV 89503

1-775-342-3561

facebook.com/charliehayesnow

charliehayes36@yahoo.com

@charliehayes77 on Twitter

Copyright 2016 Charles David Hayes, Jr.

Permission" Copies of texts may be used so long as credit and mention of this book is included.

Fast & Faster!

Introduction

This is a book about Motor Racing.

It is not a full autobiography of me; rather it's an account of my experiences of being a racing driver from 1958 through 1968. There are memory gaps for sure and sometimes doubts about chronology owing to the fact that this is being written at the rather ripe age of almost 80. So I ask the reader to allow me a few mistakes. And maybe an occasional typo! I appreciate that!

Note that some bits in the book first appeared in my 2006 book "Life After Death". They just fit in this one so I copied with no shame since I am the author of both! There is one error, in Life After Death: regarding the Mosport crash: The year was 1967, not 1968.

Hopefully this book will provide some entertainment and even fill in blanks in awareness of the events herein for many who were participants or fans at the time. If so I will be happy indeed.

With warm regards for all the great racers, and fans, and corner workers, and stewards, who might enjoy this effort.

Charlie Hayes, April 2016

Fast & Faster!

Fast & Faster!

Prologue

When I was about three, my mother asked a neighbor, "When do little boys start to walk?" The neighbor was aghast: "Isn't your son more than three?"

"Yes", my mother answered. I mean, when they stop running!?"

THAT was portent of things to come. I was always about speed, even then.

My dad was an extraordinary man who was a highly successful tax lawyer in DC. He had literally many hundreds of friends! When Pearl Harbor happened he, despite having three small children, enlisted and attained a commission as a Lt. Cdr. In the US Navy. Mother agreed; she recognized what we all learn later, that this was a man of immense loyalty to the country as well as a man of courage and deep conviction.

I would like to have had some of his pure gumption. But my courage would be more selfish as things turned out.

Dad was killed in the Navy near the end of WW2, aboard an ill-fated ship called The Indianapolis. He was not in the water like so many poor men; he was killed instantly when I was eight, in August 1945 by a torpedo from the last Japanese submarine in the Pacific Ocean. That would later haunt me....

But as we do I survived and grew, giving my mother fits along the way. As a teenager I was no less than a bratty little terrorist to her. Still bothers me 65 years later!

I grew up across the street from one Representative Carl Vinson, who now has an aircraft carrier named for him; he was chairman of the House Armed Services committee in the fifties. When I was around fifteen Representative Vinson invited me over to his porch one summer day and over iced tea told me he had made arrangements for me to become a Senate page.

There was a LOT of respect for my father in D.C. and this was but one expression of that. I had NO clue what kind of opportunity that was. I said no, thanks anyway; I would rather shoot pool and build model airplanes. Duh.

See, I was born with a silver spoon in my mouth but I spit the damn thing out. The reactive mind is a very stupid mechanism. And there was this weird sense of growing up rich UNTIL my dad was killed; then it was that the house needed painting and my mom wore a threadbare coat. Mixed signals!

Essentially, I was angry, depressed, lonely, and totally defiant of anyone who tried to talk to me about what I was becoming. My two sisters were strangers to me; the older one much later said that since I was this pissed off little demon, that we had arrived at "an armed truce". So like her!

I quit school in the eighth grade; I just got bored and real tired of repeating crap for tests I had no interest in. And at the age of fifteen, I was already drinking and doing drugs. And hanging with my black musician friends in the D.C ghettos. Playing a mediocre be-bop Jazz on Tenor Saxophone.

And driving before I had a license, drunk and high, sailing off the road at 4 AM in a friend's taxicab.

Because at that time I had no clue about cornering speeds I demolished an innocent mailbox in that little process!

A man out walking his dog (at 4 AM!) saw this and took down the license number. When the cops came knocking on the taxi driver's door he gave me up in a heartbeat. I would have done the same.

So the police arrived at my mother's house and took me in - poor mom - she was beginning to sadly realize that through NO fault of her own, she had somehow given birth to a fool.

At the police station, I'm mug-shot, fingerprinted and lectured but no record was kept. Since I was not yet old enough to drive and still considered a juvenile, I got off with a slap on the wrist.

I was becoming more and more of a total jerk, a know-it-all, and an outcast, a loner, arrested in adolescence both literally and figuratively. But I got really good at pretending to be nice, polite, happy, and socially adept. It was all an act, pasted on top of a "me" that was lonely, sad, and scared beyond belief.

An Old Married Man At Eighteen: in January of 1955, at the ripe old age of 18, I got married to a beautiful 21-year-old woman. I had fallen deeply into lust with this girl, which I thought was love. She later admitted in a moment of candor that a large part of her attraction to me was that she thought I had a lot of money. I did have some. But there was never "enough."

I remember sitting on the edge of the bed on my wedding night thinking, "What have I gotten myself INTO?" Something was wrong; I was all alone despite my very pretty bride's presence next to me in the bed.

I did not fit in anywhere. And I was on my own!

But by 1958 I had some money from a small inheritance from a favorite uncle, I am married, and a father to a kid we named Charles David Hayes II who turned out to be a really fine man we call Dave.

I was, however, NOT happy. Since I quit school about all I could be was a salesman, and somehow I got damn good at it! But to face the pretenses I lived AS, I was seeking escape from the drudgery and boredom of "day by day in this petty pace," as Shakespeare put it.

Racing cars became that escape.

Fast & Faster!

Chapter 1: 1958

When I turned 21, in 1958, I inherited a small amount of money, enough for a down payment on a Jaguar XK140 MC. A neighbor invited me to go up to Cumberland Maryland (I lived a hundred miles from there in Chevy Chase MD. at the time).

As I sat there on the side of a hill and watched a bunch of guys with Jaguars racing each other for the lead in a production car race (with SCCA, the Sports Car Club of America) I was entranced! Because I knew I could do that, and I could probably do that better than these guys were doing that.

That was the start of 11 years of very fast living. I had found a home!

So I found out what I needed to do, got a roll bar, driving suit, helmet etc. and set out for an SCCA Driving School at what would become my home track, Marlboro Maryland. To prepare for the race, I had a well-known mechanic named Steve Spitler prep the car.

The Driving School was really rudimentary; it amounted to a certified teacher riding around with me pointing out where to go. After a few races I was also a certified teacher!

He watched me as I drove around, and I, having done a great deal of practicing on the park roads around Washington DC, was standing on it right out of the gate. The teacher told me I trusted the car too much. I steadfastly ignored him and set out trying to go fast and then faster, as I figured that was obviously the point of going racing!

(I discovered a decade later that the man was correct in a way. But more on this later....)

Hell, the guy was clearly a wanker in my view anyhow. After all I had three years of racing my ass off at night in the roads of Rock Creek Park in Washington DC.

Steve was testing a D type Jaguar at the time. He came swooping by me going into a tricky turn at Marlboro called the Subway. He was a couple of hundred yards ahead; and as he disappeared around the corner I saw a cloud of dust immediately followed by track workers waving yellow flags. My heart flipped over as I slowly drove around and saw Steve lying in a heap in the road and the D Type upside down in the brush on the outside of the corner.

No seat belts. And it turned out, a cheesy old crash hat.

I made my way back to the pits and as I watched, the ambulance took off and I lit out after it in the XK140. We drove 'em to the track on the street in those days.

Fast & Faster!

I pulled up behind the bus at the local ER and as they unloaded Steve I saw his head thrashing back and forth. But he was clearly alive.

After breathing a big sigh of relief I drove back to the circuit to continue my quest to be a racing driver.

After another hour practice wrapped up and I went and found my instructor, and asked him how Steve was doing

The guy said real casually, Steve died.

I was shocked beyond belief and enraged at the guy's lack of any feeling for a sudden unexpected death there that day.

I drove home in the bluest funk imaginable. I walked in the door and startled my then wife Dottie by throwing my helmet across the room yelling "that's IT. I am DONE with this racing shit!)

Of course, the next morning I gather my stuff and drive out to Marlboro where I manage to win my very first race.

Helluva a start hunh?

I won three more races in 1958. All at Marlboro.. Man, that was a great time.

Right about here, I think it is time for a little back story. I grew up in a wealthy family, in Chevy Chase Maryland. At least they were wealthy until World War II took my dad, who was very successful tax lawyer in Washington, DC. There was still little money. However, I inherited some when I was 21. By that time, I had gorgeous wife, and a charming little boy named Charles David III as I mentioned in the Prologue. We called him Dave or David. Today he goes by Dave Hayes. Turned out to be a great guy through no fault of my own!

So I had a very interesting family, two sisters. One was older, one younger. I cannot really say we got along all that well. But hey, we managed.

But after a taste of racing, everything else fell away and it was all about the sport. But hey, I am ahead of myself.

I got married when I was 18. My wife looked like Sophia Loren! And I was devoted to her. Along the way, I had been selling home improvements for a company in Washington when I actually got recruited to a sales job at a sports car dealership, Manhattan Auto, in Bethesda, Maryland. I had also bought a small house in Kensington for my budding family. I worked on the Jag in a carport attached to the house.

In any case the job was good news! I was going to get a salary and commission, and his really stoked me given I have a family now. Plus there was the fact that I could demo sports cars around the construction of the capital Beltway. That is right; they were building the damn thing! Huge earthmovers and all.

But there was a lovely chicane at the end of a part of the Beltway that was completed, and a man did I show off the Austin Healey Sprite and other fine little sporty cars there, braking super deep and scaring the bleep out of the passengers.

I sold a lot of cars. Because I could show buyers what the cars would do.

I was pretty damn happy all things considered, even though I thought about racing all the time.

After winning my first four I was really thirsty. But hey, I knew nothing about sponsorship or any of that business stuff and had nowhere near enough money to keep going on my own.

But that would soon change.

Meanwhile, Steve's widow used to hang out in the agency because Steve had a lot of friends there. Her name was Pat and she was quite attractive. One day she came by my cubicle, sat on the desk hip wise, and started playing with a small fastener. She twirled around, grinning. Then she said "see how much fun you can have with a little screw"?

I had never been come on to so blatantly in my short life. But hey, I had a wife I loved and a little boy I cherished. No way I was going to go there. That was the first time it happened that way; it would occur again many years later with a different wife and little boy. But I have never regretted the decision to pass in both instances.

The job was good and I learned to deal with the feelings of needing to race to feel whole and complete. Then the completely unexpected happened.

More about that in the next chapter.

Chapter 2: 1959

In March of 1959, I was not thinking much about racing, though I certainly wanted to do it! But there was no funding to run the Jaguar and besides which I needed the thing for work, shoulders and all that. And the good wife was happy I had an actual job without having to go risking my neck. Plus there was my wonderful son David to think about.

But all that doubt went bye bye soon enough.

One day I was hanging out in the showroom at the agency where I was a salesman, and a young fella named John Bishop, no relation to the IMSA man and painter, came by my desk to chat, and in the course of our talk asked me if I would drive his new Austin Healey in the SCCA national championship races in Class D production. He was one of maybe 12 folks that saw me winning at Marlboro.

I think I said who do I have to kill!!

The Presidents Cup race at Marlboro MD was in April, so we had plenty of time to prepare the car, get the roll bar in, put straight pipe exhaust on, get the proper seat belts in and so on.

All the while I was going like, is this really happening? Ya know, seems too good to be true. Here I had a total of four races under my belt and I had a sponsor!

And no objections from the wife despite the tragic demise of Steve Spitler the year before.

Bloody miraculous in semi pro racing. Hell, I figured sponsorship only happened in the budding NASCAR series.

We could not take money for racing in SCCA but nowhere did it say we could not accept a personal benefactor.

Just no prize money.

Anyway we went to Marlboro with a fresh set of racing recap tires that were soft as butter. Perfect for wet weather. Good in the dry but in the wet.... dynamite.

And lo and behold it rained.

I blew off all the factory prepped Austin Healeys as well as a large covey of Corvettes. We were just stoked over the moon. Of course we won the class and went home with an outsized trophy and a ton of pride. John was really happy. So my ride was set for the season.

We next went to Virginia International Raceway for the Danville National. All I remember about that event is that my best friend Pierre Mion flipped his AC Bristol in practice and I helped pound that aluminum bodywork back into some semblance of shape for his E Production race. How or where he or I finished I simply don't remember!

Next on the calendar was Cumberland, MD, the place that originally inspired me to take on this amazing sport. Sorry but again I don't remember where or if I finished. One record says I was 15th. Rather a poor result I suppose. But I ain't sure! It was after all, some 57 years ago as of the date of this writing….

What I DO recall like it was yesterday was that at the end of the long straight there was a terrifying sheer drop of about a thousand feet. I wasn't all that sure about braking and such! But I did soldier on….

At some point we had shown well enough that BMC (British Motor cars, who manufactured the car) was interested. I think it was Marlboro that impressed them most. In any case they approached us about giving us secret trick factory bits like four wheel race type disk brakes and a blueprinted engine that a good driver could get.

No cost. And zero publicity.

Another of those who we haveta kill moments.

As the season progressed, we gave the car to Ed Brown, the magician of the BMC works, to do all the major tweaks to the engine, suspension, shocks, springs etc. and install race worthy four wheel Girling disc brakes all around. (The stock brakes had crumby front discs and rear drum brakes. Very dicey for racing.)

Ed turned that sucker into a relative rocket. I used to use the overdrive switch too. Would be running along in 3rd then flip the switch, lift off a half moment and the upshift happened! Damn near like an automatic. At longer courses I would do that in fourth gear.

Fun!

I am pretty certain that I am missing at least a couple-three races in this here 79 year old mind! The next event I now recall is Montgomery NY, an airfield circuit. I made a serious mistake there.

My friend Pierre had a relative with access to prescription medications and Pierre was rather fond of something called Dexamil. He called them go pills. I didn't really need or want 'em but to please Pierre (I could such an ass-kisser in my time) I took them. They were like being on 20 cups of Starbuckeys!

Again, huge error. Ed Brown, the BMC guy who installed all the neat shit, saw I was high on something. And THAT was it on BMC support. We were summarily ordered back to New Jersey to Ed's shops for some uninstalls!

(Ed was this unflappable guy that did not favor phones. He kept his in a desk drawer to only be withdrawn in case of dire emergency.)

The next thing I did was buy an Elva DKW engine front engine Formula Junior to race at Marlboro. I think I took the thing to Nassau but damned if I remember a thing about the week! The race car was transported to the Miami dock by a racer's racer, one Ray Heppenstall. When he found out about my invite to Speed Weeks, he offered to haul the car on his insanely long three-car single deck trailer to the dock in Miami and back home after the week for a very reasonable price.

This was awesome; I felt like a real honest to God pro race car driver, having other folks transport the car, and me in a big ole airplane! We hooked up fine with the cruise ship and set out to party, play slots (offshore gambling you know) and get rocked into slumber by the gentle seas between Miami and Nassau. Wow, I was living a dream, my friends.

Chapter 3: 1960

After a semi decent 1959 season I was happy to kick back for the winter and spring. Did not know how to keep going in the only career I would ever care about.... until fate gave me a gigantic boost! I had sold the Kensington house to allow a bit more breathing room; even made a tiny profit. We moved to an apartment adjacent to Manhattan Auto and stored the Healey in the carport there. Open to unwanted visitors, scary, but nothing bad happened.

Soon my beloved uncle Jack, a very successful Capital Hill tax attorney in Washington, passed away from a heart attack. I inherited a pretty good sum of money which I quickly decided to invest in my racing career. I would ASAP turn pro. But meanwhile I knew I needed more experience in faster cars.

I found an ad for a Ferrari two litre Testa Rossa Serial #0706. I bought it from a lovely guy in Raleigh, North Carolina named Gene Parsons; he had gotten it from a champion in class E modified, one Gaston Andrey. I bought it on a promise to the owner that when the inheritance funded I would pay for the car then. He trusted me (miracle, that!) and I paid him a month later... try that today! LOL!

Fast & Faster!

That car graced the Bethesda carport too. Miracle someone didn't get a souvenir or two off the thing. Meanwhile I took the car to Marlboro to race a regional event and was immediately super disappointed in the lack of power and speed. It was after all only a two litre engine. Good handling but slow in a straight line and no real punch off corners.

Sure, it was a lot faster than the Austin Healey. But still very insufficient for my particular mindset.

See, I had figured to go up in faster cars a step at a time. Didn't want to get over my head. But my mind was faster than the two litre TR and so I immediately started seeking a faster car. This stuff ate into my funding pretty damn seriously!

I sold that Ferrari at a loss to local driver Bob Hurt. He was on a track similar to mine with a need for speed like me. Then I got hold of Briggs Cunningham's personal Lotus 18 Formula Junior car. What a jolt that car was. Set up by Alfred Momo, an Italian wizard working on the vast Cunningham sports racing car team.

But some really lousy luck plus some personal stupidity struck around this time. I agreed to rent the Lotus to a wealth amateur racer for about 25% of what the car cost. And he wrecked it!

Paid to repair and all that but the car was never the same. So I sold that one to Bob Hurt also.

A side note: Very sadly Bob Hurt, a cool guy with money, talent and movie star good looks, was nearly killed at the Indy 500 some years later (1968) as he backed into the wall at speed. He lived but was paralyzed from the neck down.

Fate worse than dying in a racer's view....

Late in 1960 I bought an Elva Rear engine BMC powered Formula Junior mainly for Marlboro races. But then an opportunity arrived in my mailbox in the form of an "A" invitation to Nassau speed weeks. Wow. Bahamas! I loved Nassau, having been there the year before (though all I recall is sun, sand and a bumpy racetrack.) Wow. The "A" invite meant all expenses paid except food: Transport from Miami for the car plus folks, lovely hotel rooms, free parties all week, and then some good old get down car racing. Nothing better than that.

I was all over it and soon my wife Dottie, my best friend at the time Pierre Mion and I were on a Pan Am propeller plane, maybe a DC3 (this was my first ever flight and I was entranced by the sight of the clouds BELOW me!) We flew to Miami to catch the boat for Nassau, a gorgeous spot in the Caribbean a short overnight boat ride away.

Climbing off the awesome boat after a lovely night at sea (nothing like a cruise ship for a wonderful night's sleep) we arrived at a lovely bed and breakfast kind of spot called the Buena Vista, our free accommodations that came with the A invite.

Indeed the view was beautiful. The outdoor dining area was a sumptuous combination of elegant tableware and soft lighting, sultry summery breezes off the ocean, and terribly sophisticated waiters and other staff. It was like heaven. (If you saw the movie "The Firm" and remember Mitch McDeere's wife's visit to the Caymans, you will have a perfect picture of the Buena Vista's utterly Bahamian al fresco dining area.)

Pierre and Dottie soon went off and left me to study my navel in our room at the hotel. But then by some weird stroke of fate I met a beautiful young blue-eyed blonde legal secretary from Virginia who was in Nassau for a winter holiday.

Dottie was gallivanting about on a bicycle avec Pierre so I let my lust guide my actions! Kitty was her name, sex kitten was her fame.

We did not go further than heavy petting but that lady with her awesome bare upper body sent me to a whole nother kind of heaven!

Dottie and Pierre were a definite item but honestly, I did not much care. Well, maybe I was more than a little bit disturbed….

(A note to the reader here: I am very uncertain of the chronology of the events I am describing, and am especially suspicious of events at Nassau except that I am sure of what I just wrote above happening in December 1960. There are probably more than a few errors of dates; please forgive me. No doubt I took full advantage of the open bar at the many parties! In any case, the 79 year old brain is having a tough time remembering dates and so on. Sorry!)

I was unhappy in my then 5 year old marriage even though we had a charming 3 year old boy by this time. I was so bored and yet wrapped headwise in racing that I decided to take off for England where I hoped to get in on a couple of good race car buys for me and my good friend, fellow driver Jack Lyles. I was reading Autosport, the British racer's magazine, when I discovered an ad for one Ian Raby, a used race car dealer near London. I set up a meeting with him and climbed aboard a big Pan Am jet for London post haste.

Fast & Faster!

Arriving in London my biological clock was all out of whack so I ended up, after leaving DC in the AM, unable to sleep at like 8 PM UK time. I went for a long walk at Oh Dark Something on the streets near my hotel, a small, safe West End spot. Kensington, I think it was. I remember falling in love with Diesel fumes, which were wonderfully all pervasive!

Raby met me on a murky London morning and announced it was a beautiful day. Hunh? It was foggy and drizzly. I figured either this cat was nuts or maybe just acclimated from birth. Ian bundled me into some sedan or other and off we went to a marvelous race course near London in Kent, Brands Hatch.

At Brands I found that Raby had brought a couple of cars for me to try out so I set about learning the short version of the course (the longer course was at that time only used for Grand Prix racing.) I loved this little circuit right off! Especially nifty was the first turn, called Paddock Bend, which was a speedy 100 mph downhill off camber right that bottomed out and then swept uphill to a 180 degree right called Druids. Big old trees at apex! All vary British, that lot!

This was all happening, thanks to Ian, on a Wednesday, a regular day for open practice. I met Frank Nichols of Elva Cars that day and he offered me his new rear engine car, the Mark VI if memory is correct. That little sucker was quick!

Then a bit later that day I met John Copper of Cooper race cars, who introduced me to a young fellow from Scotland who, I learned, had just won something like 23 of 24 Formula Three races and was rather highly thought of (ya think!?) by the assembled racers.

His name was Jackie Stewart! Now SIR Jackie.

Walt Hansgen was also there that day, a great driver from America who was having a go with one of John Cooper's cars. I remember him referring to the car as his "office" and as his time on circuit approached quipped "time to go to work!" What a neat guy.

I had a partner for racing back in Maryland named Jack Lyles and ultimately I bought two Lotus 18s from Raby for us. I went back home after a very satisfying trip to England, and had a welder I liked do up a double decker trailer. We picked up the cars off the boat from the UK in Baltimore and set off to Marlboro to beat the boredom of being by going blinking quick in these two nifty little race cars!

Mind you, as I write this much of the year 1960 is still blurry after 56 years! But I will keep giving it a shot because I really want to honestly share as much as I can of the incredible roller coaster called Motor Racing!

Other highlights include a drive or two in that noisy, smelly Elva DKW front engine Formula Junior. I remember running at Marlboro and Nassau but the rest is a mystery today.

I also recall buying an Elva BMC rear engine Formula Junior from the master salesman and later fine racer Charlie Kolb in a weak moment up in Manhattan. Clearly at times there was more money than common sense. But we took the car to Nassau where I met two incredible guys and champion drivers, Taffy (Wolfgang) von Trips and no less than (now Sir) Stirling Moss. Taffy was horribly killed in the Formula One race that made Phil Hill world champion (talk about mixed emotions!) And thankfully, as of the writing Sir Stirling is going strong!

Incidentally Stirling and I hit it off and would become faster friends (pun intended!) in Nassau in 1961 and for years later when we would meet. More about that later....

One of the things that happened that year is that I had received that nice inheritance from a beloved uncle. He had passed from a heart attack, that's in the family. Mom died of it and I as of this writing (April 2016) have Chronic Heart Failure too.

In any event one thing led to another and I found myself one fine sunny day up from DC to New York City at Luigi Chinetti's West Side (54th & 11th Avenue) Ferrari Emporium.

Fast & Faster!

Having sold my two litre Ferrari, I was definitely in the market for a faster car... fast is good, but I always wanted to go faster!

Luigi had a pontoon fender 250 TR Testa Rossa which I decided I had to have. Having enough money to actually buy it was a blessing! I reckon at this stage I did have a bit more cash than talent....

So I snapped the gorgeous thing up and took it to Marlboro, and did okay; I think I won a couple of regional races with it. I remember quite well the ecstatic sound of that straight-piped V12 engine though! It was better than a Mozart symphony or a Charlie Parker riff, to my ears.

Then I decided to go to Thompson, Connecticut for a national SCCA race. In practice, the engine dropped a valve. Ug! Shocking as hell, given I had never over-revved it. So I went back to Luigi with the car and said I didn't think it was my fault. Luigi said if he could confirm that, he would rebuild the engine at no charge.

I was thoroughly intimidated by Luigi. He was this larger than life figure with a background in motor racing that included a twenty three hour drive at Le Mans that led to overall victory. And here he was surrounded by about a million Ferraris!

Who DOES that!?

Fast & Faster!

Luigi had two great mechanics, who also became friends, Alberto and Alfredo. They examined the engine and determined I had indeed not over-revved it.

And so, Luigi rebuilt the engine for me at no charge. That was a class act!

I have never forgotten what a gentleman and true racer Luigi was. And his son is in the same bloodline. Great people, great racers. A privilege to know them.

A brief aside: the writing of this book is dredging up some rather uncomfortable memories, to say the least. I am reliving some really dumb decisions around the inherited money issue, and gutting up nasty feelings and experiences. And I just feel like I am showing up like a damn fool and that ain't so good an emotional state!

But I am committed to telling the real thing as best I can rather than trying to come off like some bright star. So if I look stupid so be it. If the shoe fits.....

So…onward!

Chapter 4: 1961

In the spring of '61 I put an ad in the fine rag "Competition Press" for the Testa Rossa, now painted white. I'd been driving the thing on the street on dealer tags and more than one pissed off and/or jealous guy had yelled insults at me. Sheesh!

I got one call off the ad; no less than Carl Haas. His feats in racing are now legend. But at that time he was selling Elvas out of a tiny showroom on Chicago's north side. Across the street there resided an entrepreneur named Wayne Burnett and Carl was getting the car for him.

On the come I towed to Chicago from Maryland; there was this thing about Carl, I somehow knew I could trust him to buy the car as long I had represented it honestly, which I had. We consummated the deal in a gorgeous garden type restaurant on the north side of Chicago, right on the lake.

Carl is an absolute gentleman. I know there are stories to the contrary but he was always nothing but great with me. Honest, open, heart on his sleeve. Not many people know he had a dear friend who was hooked on drugs (I don't mean racing which I was definitely addicted to).... no this guy had it bad. Heroin, I believe. And Carl took care of his every need and supported him through painful rehab.

Fast & Faster!

I will never forget Carl; he turned out to be one of my best and longest term friends ever. We lost touch but the heart connection is still there to this day.

Harry Heuer, a great racer who also knew Carl, commented on Facebook as this chapter was being written:

"Charlie, the restaurant might have been at the old Edgewater Beach Hotel. Carl (Shakey) Haas, Wayne Burnett, Harry Woodnorth, Ernie Ericson, Tossi Alex, and a couple other Chicago drivers whose names I am having trouble remembering right now used to hang out there. We swapped stories, laughed, played gin, had lunch and tried to stick Shakey with the check. You are right. Carl is a man to ride the river with."

He of course is correct on all counts!

Using the money from the sale I tried to sell a few cars in a small building in Bethesda Maryland. This venture also failed rather quickly but along that short path I ended up with a 250GT Ferrari Coupe; not a very popular car. So I set up a trade in late May with exotic car emporium owner Bob Grossman, also a Ferrari racer, in Nyack NY to purchase Ferrari 250GT #2237, a Short Wheelbase Berlinetta. It was a brilliant Red Burgundy metallic job and was the Paris show car. Only problem was the fuel filler; more about that item later.

I discovered recently that Grossman had raced the car twice before selling it to me. Had I known that I likely would not have bought the thing; I'd have gone to Luigi Chinetti instead. But Bob did not tell me. That was in my view a certain lack of integrity that would show up later with this guy. But not knowing, I did the deal for the 250GT SWB and set out to drive it back to Maryland from New York.

I was blown away by how smooth the car felt. It was like being on a Caribbean beach with the sound of a gentle surf steadily thrumming. Paradise! SO beautiful to hear the soft insistent sound of that 3 Litre V12. Indescribably delicious. I remember floating down the New Jersey Turnpike like I was in a dream. Ecstatic. I was in love with a car!

Once home I started looking for places to race this beauty. It was, after all, much more than a street ride! I found a National race near Chicago at Elkhart Lake, Wisconsin. I called Carl Haas to see if had inside tips on where to say and so on. There was going to be not only a sprint race I could run in but also a 500 Kilometer race (300 Miles) which a co-driver could be enlisted for. Carl told me about it asked me if in return for a new set of Goodyear Racing Tires he could be my co-driver.

Fast & Faster!

There was, as I said, something about the guy. I found myself agreeing on the spot!

I had a casual friend that was a racing fan, named Bill. I asked him if he would like to go with me to the race and be a crew guy for the 500K. He agreed and off we went to Chicagoland. What a fun drive that was and we were not even racing yet. Well maybe a little!

We pulled in and settled in a motel across from the Edgewater and met up with some other racers from back east. I was steadfastly ignoring the fact that I had a wife who was pregnant out to here at home; I could NOT be bothered. I was gonna RACE! Basically I forgot about her (we were not really getting along at that point so it was terribly easy to put her out of my mind.)

We all went out for a meal, and though I was not drinking because we were going to race, I was still a bit nuts. There was a foxy lady with one of the other guys, and when we got back to our rooms I grabbed her by the hand and we left everyone in the dust and reeled into the room I was sharing with Bill, who was sound asleep. Never knew why he went to bed so early.

The lady and I immediately tore each other's clothes off and had at it, waking Bill up in the process. He was, to put it mildly, shocked. (Hell so was I. A bit guilty too.) This was the first time I would be unfaithful.

But man the sex was awesome!

The next day was a gorgeous sunny one and off we all went to Elkhart, Carl and I had arranged to meet there. We got the racing tires on and I set out to practice and learn the four mile circuit, having suppressed all traces of guilt about the night before (but that guilt and shame for what I had done would erupt later!)

When I thought about that night with The Fox, I felt like the worst asshole in the world but the racing dulled the sensations and I managed a fast time in the SWB. Carl was quite quick as well. Racing took me over and I barely thought about my awful behavior the rest of the weekend.

I won the sprint race easily, and when I arrived at the restaurant afterward Carl said "Here comes the man of the hour." See, I want you all to know, I was no hero. Just a flawed human trying to have the best time of my life, regardless. And Bill was barely speaking to me, though he was doing what needed to be done on the car, polishing it and caring for it. I knew he was pissed but didn't know what to do. I was being aloof, a "hero driver" in my mind. Sheesh!

Well, enough about that for now. There would be hell to pay later but at this point I focused on the racing and let everything else drop away as Carl and I got set for the 500K.

We got pole position for the Elkhart Lake 500 K with the SWB car easily and had the laconic Bill in place to crew for the driver swap and refueling. I would start and then give the car to Carl around 1/3 of the way. But we ran into a problem that ought to have been anticipated but had been ignored: the fuel filler.

The car came equipped with a big 6" diameter fuel filler cap. Great for refueling, right? Problem was, it necked down into a crooked tight little pipe in the trunk. I suppose that was for luggage space, after all this WAS a show car!

So it seemed like an hour to fill the damn thing with gas (though it was likely 2-3 minutes). In any case it was enough to give our competitors the Corvettes and insurmountable lead. I was pretty pissed though Carl didn't seem too upset. But later I found he too was thoroughly frustrated, he just didn't show it publicly.

I don't remember where we finished. I think we were third overall. It was first in Class A Production of course but that was meaningless. We had the fastest car! Frustration is not near a strong enough word. Some choice four-letter ones come to mind here!

But as with all awful experiences (and this was nowhere as bad as some to come later) we got over it and went on the next event. However, before we raced again there was some nasty karma to deal with at home.

My wife gave birth to Roger Craig Hayes while I was on the road! Pierre Mion stepped up and took care of her thank God. What an embarrassment it was all around.

Dottie moved into her own apartment with Pierre's help shortly after Roger was born. I sold the fine house I had paid a small fortune for at a loss and gave Dottie a bunch of money which she asked for and got through a shrewd local racer and attorney, Herb Gussin. I was glad to be released from what had become a loveless kind of prison. Again not my finest hour….

Dottie told me much later that Pierre was royally pissed at me for leaving her in the lurch like that. Understandable!

Roger (I think Roger Penske inspired the name; I was not around for that occurrence of labeling the boy) but who knows! Never asked either Dottie or Pierre. There was bad news right from the git-go: that poor kid had a birth defect called Childers's Disease. He would never develop beyond infancy.

I am ashamed to admit I had nothing to do with his care. Dottie was a hero taking care of that boy. She even got NIH to look at the kid to see if anything could be done. Mercifully for all concerned the lad died at about age two. And had never developed at all, sadly.

I could not attend the funeral; in my secret heart I thought Pierre was the father since he and Dottie had been spending a LOT of time together and he seemed much closer to her than I ever was.

(Much later I asked Dottie and she said I was indeed the father. That felt even more shameful. I had ignored my own son. In a moment of candor she also admitted she had married me for the money. Drastic!)

I had opened a small sports car repair shop. That ate into the inheritance big time and turned out to be two mistakes: Dottie left me and ended up with my (former) best friend Pierre Mion (tad bit of betrayal there, wrecked my gut and trust in Human Beings for a damn good while!)

There was a rather costly divorce, and the business failed for lack of customers. And I sold the big beautiful house for a significant loss, of course. Thanks so much Dorothy Marie!

Fast & Faster!

So I was kind of left with seriously depleted funding to build my racing career. I cannot believe the stupid mistakes I made. Pisses me off! How could I have been so stupid? Never mind, it's a rhetorical question! As life unfolded I proved to be NOT a good businessman....

But in the process I got a Maryland used car dealer's license which came in real handy over the next couple of years! Would have been costly to buy tags for a Ferrari.

Anyway, I moved into a small apartment near Bethesda and parked my Ferrari on the street outside. Imagine doing that today around there. The wheels and steering wheel and logos would have disappeared in one night!

As to the rest of 1961 and 1962 there is a lot of memory loss. I looked up the history of the Berlinetta, Serial #2237GT, and some of it seems off according to my memory but I am going to mostly go with the official record and fill in as much as I am able to.

Okay, dropped a little Gingko Biloba so here goes....

I do remember going to Thompson, Connecticut in the latter part of 1961 and winning the race, beating the nemesis Corvettes in the process. That was great fun; I enjoyed the Thompson road course and was very gratified to beat Mr.

Fast & Faster!

Grossman! I also won at Lime Rock and Bridgehampton according to the record but I do not recall and details of those events....

One thing I remember clearly is our racing, and the parties and beach times, in Nassau in 1961. I had met Stirling Moss the year before and was quite happy to see him turn up with his Rob Walker SWB Ferrari 250GT. We would race together!

Not only that, we had rooms next to each other at the great Nassau Beach Lodge, complimentary luxury suites given the drivers through the efforts of the promoter of the Nassau events, Captain Sherman (Red) Crise. Great guy that! We got an A invitation which meant all was paid by the promoters except air fare. The cars were even shipped over to the island, along with those who chose the boat rather than via air, for free. This was an amazing deal. Red Crise could rival Bernie Ecclestone if he were alive now!

The parties were amazing, with open bars and great snacks we could make dinner out of. All part of the deal.

I recall fellow racer Peter Bryant elbowing his way up to a jam packed bar shouting in his delightful British accent, "Just give us a bottle of Scotch and a bucket of water and we'll make do!" Hilarious!

December was not the high season in Nassau so all these promotions were designed to get folks back during the peak times. Sure must have worked. In any event we had a ball there! My dear friend Kitty had joined me there for the week of events and we of course shared a room.... the one next to Stirling's. Boy does that bring back fond memories! And one bizarre one:

There was this fellow from DC that had the most expensive MG TD ever raced at Marlboro. I recall he was a photographer with a strange penchant: visiting the room where Kitty and I were staying he suggested, when he observed Kitty looking very attractive indeed, that he could stick around a take a few choice photos. I kicked his ass out at once.

Kitty was a sophisticated, gorgeous blonde with a well-honed wit and she just loved our sexual escapades. Of course I did too.

Once upon a time during late 1961 Kitty and I had gone up to New York to Le Chanteclair, the fine French restaurant at 18 East 49th that belonged to champion driver Rene Dreyfus and his brother Maurice. The place had pictures of racing drivers from all over the world; mine was there as well. The bartender, Jimmy, asked Kitty what she would like to drink. "Scotch", she said. "Water?" Jimmy asked. "No", Kitty said. "I never touch it. Fish fuck in it."

So dry and natural. The whole area went deathly silent, then erupted in joyous laughter! I will never forget that precious lady!

Back to Nassau: (Now SIR) Stirling was going past our room and it seemed he had x-ray vision. As Kitty and I were enjoying an interlude of sex, Stirling rapped the window and announced "I see you in there!" we laughed but I also double checked that the blinds had been closed. They were! What a wonderful friend Stirling turned out to be. Here was this world class driver and gentleman being friendly with little old me. That was one of those times over which one never gets.

All the while, in between parties there was some racing to do. Stirling announced he had changed his own spark plugs in his Berlinetta, identical to mine except it was right hand drive,. That was no mean feat! The plugs, buried in the V12 recesses of the cylinder heads, were a bear to get at, but he managed. He had no mechanic there; neither of us did. This was party time with occasional motor racing you see. I flat loved it!

On the day of the Tourist Trophy race for GT cars, Stirling strolled over as we suited up for the event and said, "What do you say we put on a bit of a show for the people?" He suggested we swap the lead back and forth for a lap or there, then just let whoever was quickest show their stuff. I immediately agreed though I knew full well it would ONLY be a show; Stirling was of course a lot quicker than I was at my best.

The flag dropped and off we went, trading places as planned. But I actually started to think I COULD race him. Right about then he pulled up beside me to my left, under braking at the end of the straight behind the pits. We could have shaken hands; I had Left Hand drive and his was Right Hand drive. He winked, waved and disappeared. In a single lap he was out of sight.

Driving lessons on offer here, no charge! He might have quipped.

I only finished fourth. But I didn't care. I learned more from Sir Stirling Moss in that three laps than in my previous three years of driving racing cars…. how to brake really late without locking up a wheel, turning in still light on the brakes. Clipping the apex late and getting power on early. Using every bloody INCH of race track. All the while picking out some in the stands and waving at them. Incredible skills and an outgoing, cheerful and pleasing personality. Wow. He was and still is a hero to me.

So now it is on the memories of 1962....

Chapter 5: 1962

Then it was on to Marlboro for an SCCA National at my home circuit!

The unofficial record of my Ferrari Berlinetta #2237 shows that I did not finish at the Marlboro SCCA National in April 1962. Here is why: I got punted by the guy I bought my car from, the incredibly aggressive (for sports car amateur racing) Bob Grossman. He cleverly aimed his RF wheel at my LR wheel as I was accelerating out of the left hand hairpin corner; I was leading the race from the start and was full on the gas when he pulled his dirty NASCAR style trick and the rev counter (AKA Tachometer) shot off the scale. Shortly after the engine blew a piston and that was the reason for the DNF.

I guess Grossman could not stand being beaten fair and square.

I protested but since there was no visible body damage it was disallowed. Grossman of course pled innocence. Indeed he was a Gross man! (LOL). But interestingly, many years later, he bragged and chuckled about the foul to a local New York reporter and word got back to me. So much for racer's integrity. Of course I am no one to talk integrity, but on the race track I ran clean and my own conscience in that domain is clear as the sky above.

Incidentally, as of this writing there is a persistent but completely untrue rumor that I punched Bob Grossman because of the shunt. NOT true as I said; some idea of a spectator I suppose. But that was just NOT my style.

Nevertheless, that engine blown setback cost us not only a small fortune in parts – my friend Gordon Tatum and I rebuilt the engine ourselves – it also cost me a start at Danville and a loss of points toward the SCCA A Production championship from both events. I did get to Cumberland (see chapter two for how scary THAT place could be) and won there. Later came Bridgehampton; we got a good second there, although if I recall correctly arch rival Grossman won....

A little back story: I was as mentioned before parking the Ferrari outside my flat on the street that winter, after Nassau.. That I got really lucky with. The car bore the wails of winter well and meanwhile I was dating Kitty and man, we were having a GOOD time! Drinking, playing, loving it, the season passed quicker than I thought it would, given the gap between races. Thanks, Kitty dear!

Anyway, the next thing we would do was the June race at home, Les Six Heures de Marlboro. A six hour enduro. I had a good friend in town that had flown Corsairs off carriers in WW2 and was a fine Porsche driver currently, the good man

Gene Hobbs. (Aside: Gene had counseled me over and over to put some of my inheritance away for safe keeping. Of course in my infinite wisdom I ignored that advice!) Anyway, I figured he knew how to go quick AND keep the ride in one piece.

We had a proper LeMans start, wherein I ran across to the car, belted in and took off. I led the first lap and every lap thereafter until I came in at the 2 hour mark to give over to Gene, while Gordon did the painfully slow refueling job (see chapter three for why it was so slow). Gene did a master's job for his two hour stint, easily maintaining our lead over those nasty 'Vettes!

I cruised the last two hours and we won overall easily. And as my friend who was there Steve Lloyd reminded me, we also won the "Index of Performance", an award started by the organizers of LeMans that favored the smaller cars. We were nothing if not efficient!

That Ferrari was a wicked quick and reliable motor car and we were very pleased, Gordon and I, that the engine had performed flawlessly. (At one point, to make Cumberland, we had worked through like forty hours straight. I was so inspired that sleep became an option rather than a necessity).

The season after that is a blur in my mind. The record showed we ran at Nassau in #2237 but that is flat wrong; In Nassau I drove the Bill McKelvey/NART 250GTO Ferrari #3223. So much for internet accuracy eh? More about how the North American racing Team assignment there came about follows later....

I took the car to a race at Vineland, New Jersey and won easily. But some freak put sugar in the gas tank; the fancy Monza cap had no lock. Finally parking on the street (actually outside my motel room) cost me, but good. I found out about that when I started the car the next morning to drive home and found a VERY sluggish engine that ran not well at all. Somehow I knew what had happened and I was heartbroken. How could anyone DO that!?

In any case I called a Ferrari mechanic in New York and arranged to limp up to his shop. Expensive one, that. But he rebuilt the engine perfectly and so I went onward and upward, racing again at Elkhart Lake in September where I again won.

But my old friends Alberto and Alfredo from Luigi Chinetti's place were there wrenching a NART car and told me the horrible news that Taffy Trips had been killed that day at Monza in the Italian Grand Prix. Mixed emotions? Hell yes:

My fellow American Phil Hill had captured the World Championship in Formula One. I was sad as hell about Taffy but for Phil obviously pleased. That, my friends is Motor Racing.

I sold the Berlinetta to one Bob Stelloh who lived in Illinois somewhere around late September of 1962, and gave myself solace for no race car by renting an incredibly beautiful 11th floor apartment overlooking DC's National (Now Reagan) Airport, the monuments and the capitol. Amazing place, I had a party for racers and the excellent Corvette driver Dick Thompson showed up, He remarked, "this place must be a real trap". I said nothing. I had broken up with Kitty and had NO ladies in my life. But I smiled as if I had. Phony I was!

I took a job selling Chevy trucks in Arlington, VA and man did I hate that gig, but I felt I needed to somehow make some cash as my inheritance was dwindling.

I was a racer with no race car. And that really did suck.

But then one day my phone rang. It was Ivo Brillo, Luigi Chinetti's right hand man at the US Ferrari team, NART (North American Racing Team). Ivo said "Mr. Chinetti wants to know if you will drive a Ferrari 250GTO at Bridgehampton."

Yes, that WAS one of those who do I have to kill moments!

Fast & Faster!

I quit my despicable job at the Chevrolet dealer in a heartbeat and got myself up to New York post freaking haste. What a fabulous opportunity this was, to drive a works Ferrari. But like it seems was always the case, there was a bit of a catch.

I didn't find out until later I would have a co-driver – for a 400 KM (240 mile) race. I considered that completely unnecessary, of course. I had already made a key mistake in having my good friend Carl Haas co-pilot the Berlinetta at Elkhart; in retrospect I would have declined Carl's request. But in this case there was no choice.

See, the car was actually owned by a great guy named Bill McKelvey, whose very close friend was the distance driver Ed Hugus.

Look: you would never meet a nicer guy than Ed. A handsome man with an elegant pencil-thin mustache, Ed was the picture of a European hero driver! But in truth I was like two full seconds faster in the GTO at the bridge.

This was an opportunity for a sure loss to Bob Grossman in another GTO. But honest injun IF I HAD known he setup before I arrived there I still would have gone for it. Obviously! It was the FERRARI team. Duh…. Every racing driver's dream is to be called upon to drive a Ferrari.

As it transpired, Grossman took the lead and honestly he was quicker in the suicidally fast downhill right hand off camber 120 MPH turn at the end of the pit straight. Bob was not only a very good driver; he also had vast experience at The Bridge and was able to lead me without a lot of extra effort. Give the devil his due.

So as ordered I came in after pestering Grossman, even passing him or so I thought. Bob did say later he had let me by since he knew Hugus would be taking over and would be a lot slower. I fought the statement publicly; to tell the truth I or my ego did NOT want to accept that Bob really WAS faster than I was at Bridgehampton.

That did my reputation no good amongst the elite of the revered Road Racing Driver's Club (the like of Grossman and Mark Donohue, and Walt Hansgen, were members.) I really wanted in to the RRDC but my character at the time nixed that and I was never invited. I heard I was considered and voted down. Ego busted!

In any event we managed a third overall and second (to Bob Grossman) in class. Not so bad for a first outing for the team. The ever laconic Chinetti seemed satisfied so I had made my bones in a way and there would be more invitations to come from NART.

By the way I said once, "I had a long conversation with Luigi Chinetti. He said hello." Great man of few words indeed. He was all action, that guy.

Next up was the Nassau Speed Weeks for 1962 and voila! Another invite from Luigi Chinetti to drive 3223GT there. Talk about being stoked!

I LOVE Nassau. The crystal clear blue water, The swaying palm trees. The friendly natives. The amazing shopping and clubs on Bay Street. The music; oh gawd the music! And in December, the near perfect weather (well, mostly. There was rain....) Driving the race cars on the streets and roads of the island. The parties. Oh gawd, the parties!

The Nassau course was on an obsolete airfield called Oakes Field (named for the island's British Governor I believe) and traversed 4.5 miles of bumpy concrete interspersed with tropic weeds in spots, which became very challenging in the rain, which being Nassau happened from time to time. Unpredictably. As luck unfolded it rained for my event, the Nassau Trophy on Sunday. But also unpredictably that GTO handled really great in the wet; stuck like glue until I broke it loose in controlled drifts, stayed where I wanted it. What an awesome experience it was to drive that fantastic car for the equally fantastic Luigi Chinetti.

My partner in the car for Nassau was a marvelous Italian driver by the name of Lorenzo Bandini. Yes, THAT Bandini. We met in Miami a week before and had a great time; Lorenzo and I hit it off straight away and I cemented the friendship by escorting him the Miami Playboy Club. The Bunnies all just fell in love with him! It was easy to see why; he was charming, handsome like a movie star, authentic as all get-out, and spoke English very well indeed!

Writing this, I am nearly overcome with sadness and a deep sense of loss. Bandini was my absolute best friend in racing at that time, and when he was later tragically and brutally killed at Monaco racing for Ferrari in the Grand Prix there I was shocked beyond belief. I boycotted ABC and Wide World of Sports for years thereafter for showing in gruesome detail Lorenzo's burning upside down race car with him trapped inside. Lousy thrill seekers.

But at Nassau we of course had no idea or even ever entertained the thought that such things could happen to us. In our minds we were all immortal. Pedro Rodriguez, Nino Vaccarella, Mark Donohue, Masten Gregory, Bob Grossman, all these great sportsmen who thought nothing of risking their very lives for the ecstasy of racing at huge speeds; these were my friends and I was proud to be associated with them all.

Driving in the rain seemed totally natural to me; I was blissed out to toss that fine piece of automotive art about with abandon. There was no fear; the car was just that good. And my friends Alberto and Alfredo had prepared the car impeccably, as always. Those guys were artists too.

We did well, finishing the main event Nassau Trophy race 6th overall and first in class! I felt like I had finally found my true place in life: in a race car on a race track, preferably a road course as I loved turning both left AND right. Always thought of that as a bigger challenge than left turning oval tracks, but that was my personal take. Others may have disagreed but I really didn't care!

Going home I felt whole and satisfied and knew that somehow I would do this racing stuff until I dropped. Or so I felt then....

Chapter 6: 1963

My home circuit, Marlboro Raceway, had a truly oddball event every January, dubbed (appropriately) The Refrigerator Bowl. There would be various regional races, hopefully not in a snowstorm. In 1963 I met my friend Mark Donohue there; Mark had brought his Low Line Elva Formula Junior, a good looking ride from the well regarded shops of Frank Nichols of Rye, England.

Mark and I had met on the overnight boat trip to Nassau and hit it off straight away. It is no accident that his nickname was Captain Nice as he progressed in our sport. Cool guy! He introduced me to his then fiancée Sue on the boat. He would comment to me, "Isn't she neat?" I readily agreed.

The night before the races at Marlboro was for me, a party night. I wasn't scheduled to drive so I may have a few! I don't recall if Mark was imbibing but since he was to drive the Formula Junior the next day, I doubt it. Anyway we got into a weird conversation that ended up with me writing Mark a check for the Elva! Man that was unexpected and also dumb and dumber. I was in no shape to drive the car Sunday but hey, I never did much let good sense stop me.

So come Sunday I am suiting up when the SCCA official in charge came to me and asked me if I had been drinking. I suppose I still partially reeked. Of course I said NO! Of course not. Hey it was a little bit true; I had not been drinking that MORNING....!

I did drive the car that day. Don't remember where I finished by I suspect it was Dead Last. In any case the stewards never should have allowed me to compete as I had taken no practice in the car. But things were pretty loose in those days.

At least I kept the thing off the walls and was able to take it home to race another day. I even managed a third place, pretty good all things considered.

But truth to tell I hated that car.

I went to Sebring in March for the twelve hour with no car to drive. But I showed up, helmet bag in my grip, to see what happened. The first thig was to check in to the medic tent just in case I could get on board with someone. I knew the doctor in charge, which was sort of lucky because when he checked my blood pressure it was up to like 180 over 105! This however didn't daunt the doc; he had me rest lying down for fifteen minutes then took it again and was down to about 160 over 85 and he passed me to race. That was interesting and was a sign of things to come later.

There were no openings but just in case I hung out at the NART Ferrari pits. Figured I had nothing to lose. But nada. Zip. Zilch. Then good luck struck. I was invited by Mr. Chinetti to drive 250GT #3327 in the twelve hour there in; we were having a lot of fun, and I much enjoyed the fact that my friend Carl Haas was on the team as well. But I lost the shifter on a remote part of the course! Traipsing back to the pits for tools and then trekking back out to the car cost us many laps. I managed to fix the thing somehow, but the race was over for us. We finished a lousy 34th!

I raced that Elva Formula Junior a few more times, including a 110 degree hot day in Kansas, where my good friend Tucker Conley went with to share towing chores, and also a race at Danville, Virginia, which I managed to win, and even one at Lime Rock in Connecticut. But no real joy. The car so did not fit me; I never even came close to getting comfortable in it!

Give me a Ferrari any time over these flimsy uncomfortable little things!

Luigi Chinetti did not call for me to drive the GTO #3223 at Daytona; they had Fireball Roberts, the great NASCAR driver, field the car for the 300 in February. But I was called to do Sebring and was overjoyed to get back in the car there.

Unfortunately the car lost brakes and went off, narrowly missing a covey of spectators up against a flimsy snow fence. That was a moment all right. I don't remember exactly where we ended up but I heard it was 18th overall. Not exactly my best showing.

But a very good thing happened that spring! I met my wife Evey and I knew she was "the one" for me. We dated casually, then seriously, then in August we got married and had an amazing honeymoon in Nassau. August in Nassau was rather hot and humid but we could have cared less: we were ecstatic and had a blast on the island.

I must admit this is not fun to write because due to some really dumbass actions on my part years later Evey and I parted ways in a civil but to me terrible divorce. Which I stupidly asked for because she was having a long standing affair. But I was at fault on that business as well. It's complicated but as far as I am concerned Evey was and still is a lady. Period full stop.

I still feel like she was THE love of my life and it is tough to admit I screwed up and lost her.... Like I have said before writing all this stuff up is dredging up some deep emotional pains. We had so many GOOD years together....

Evey (or as some say, Evie) and I made a great team. She did the lap charts and scoring and was always right on. She was a banker when we met and she had great intellectual skill and a big warm heart. I miss her awfully.

Back to the racing; I sold the Elva F Junior but I don't recall exactly to whom or when. Then I heard from Bill McKelvey who wanted to acquire a sports racing car and had done a deal with Joe Huffaker in San Francisco to buy his Super Genie Ford that Pedro Rodriguez was racing at the Laguna Seca pro race in October.

The great part was that he wanted me to drive it!

Evey and I towed an empty trailer using Bill's station wagon out to Monterey, where we enjoyed the race, meeting some old pals like Roger Penske, Timmy Mayer and Augie Pabst there.

There is nothing like a round trip across country to foster intimacy. Evey and I really bonded on that trip. It was – she was – so sweet it hurt.

We arrived back in Maryland with the Genie in time to freshen up the 289 Ford motor and make an appearance at Marlboro for a regional SCCA race. I remember prepping the car vividly:

while I was at a fellow named Warren Shamlian's shop I got a phone call from Bill McKelvey informing that President Kennedy had been killed. I will never forget the immense sadness and sense of loss Bill and I experienced together on that call. JFK was the first President I ever voted for and I could not imagine who would do such a thing, or why. All the aftershocks and stories that followed left me numb. But racing called, as usual!

I believe we DNF'd at Marlboro; we went next to Nassau for Speed Weeks. I looked up the results and it seems we ended up 60th! I recall nothing from that week except for the fact that the love of my life was with me and at that stage of our marriage that really counted!

But 1964 would bring a whole new chapter in "Chargin' Charlie's" career.

Chapter 7: 1964

Daytona was first up with the Genie; again I don't remember what happened there but I DO recall meeting a guy named Larry Tomaris, who told me that Chicagoan Carl Haas and his friend, Porsche dealer Oliver Schmidt, were starting up a team of Elva-Porsches and there was a seat open. He said I could get the ride and all the maintenance, travel, entry fees and other racing expenses would be taken care of. But there was just one small catch: I had to buy the car.

Well, Evey and I talked it over and together decided that since I had the required funds left over from my inheritance it would be a wise career move. So I went for it, and simultaneously started a serious exercise program to lose a bunch of weight and get really fit. It worked; before the first race at Augusta GA I dropped about 30 unnecessary pounds and felt better than I ever had in life. Man, I was soooo ready!

Meanwhile Graham Shaw asked me to drive his Cobra at Sebring. That was a blast! I made a great LeMans start and jumped out in front – for about 3 seconds – but it was fun while it lasted. A while later I was motoring down a back straight when I saw a wheel rolling off by itself. I thought, well some nitwit lost a wheel!

Then I braked for a right hand bend and the front end of MY Cobra dropped down and I was riding on a brake disc! I limped back to the pits but our twelve hour race was cut to one hour and that was that. I went home with Evey and stepped up my exercise program, which had already shown good results: running across the track for the LeMans start at Sebring proved easy and invigorating.

On the pleasant and enjoyable trip driving to Augusta for our first USRRC event with the Elva Porsche team, we got the horrible news that Timmy Mayer had gotten killed practicing for a race in Australia. I couldn't believe it! Timmy was fast and smart and never reckless. I heard that he hit the only tree around when he went off in his Cooper F1 car – he was on Bruce McLaren's team and was a definite "comer". Damn sad day that was.

I had bought a used 1961 Cadillac convertible, white with red leather for $2800 the year before! $2800. Probably $40,000 in today's money.

Anyway that was just a really great way to travel in 1964. We arrived in Augusta well rested and went to breakfast with teammate Chuck Dietrich; Chuck's wife Suzy remarked that I looked good, noting that I had lost a lot of weight since we last saw each other in Daytona in early February. I was pleased but

I also knew she was not going to be happy come qualifying as I was very confident I would be faster than Chuck. And indeed I was.

The Elva Porsche felt right to me at once. The car handled so well I could throttle-push into controlled drifts at any speed and there was plenty of horsepower, especially for an under two litre car. The torque was good too and I felt completely at home on the up and down twisty course.

Practice went smoother than expected and qualifying was a slam dunk for n\first under two litre; I actually put the car fourth overall in front of a slew of big V8 engined cars! VERY satisfying. And as far as I was concerned Evey was bringing me great good fortune.

Being in love AND being fast – doesn't get any better than that.

Oliver and Carl had put together an amazing crew also. The guys worked their butts off to make sure these fragile cars would be as reliable as possible but there were to be failures of various components over the course of the season. However for this event the car was bulletproof.

As the race unfolded I jumped out to a big lead over Chuck Dietrich in the second fastest under two litre, he was in another

Fast & Faster!

Elva Porsche as mentioned before. Nice guy, good driver so I was really pleased to be quicker than he was.

Then the rocks hit the gourd.

A great driver named Harry Heuer was in a Meister Brau beer sponsored Chaparral 1, a demon quick front engined car with a big V8. I had gotten ahead of some of these cats because I made a start worthy of Daddy Don Garlits in a dragster but these bigger cars started reeling me in as the event progressed.

Harry came up behind me and attempted to get by but as Harry would put it later, my race car got VERY Wiiide! He finally darted through in the inside of a fast left hander, but in so doing he ran his left rear wheel off onto a gravelly shoulder and threw a boulder back at precisely the perfect angle to hit me right upside the head (no full helmets in those days.)

I was knocked sideways and damn near passed out! I motored on woozily, and I remember wondering if I would have to call it quits, but after a lap or two I was still crawling along (relatively speaking) when Dietrich pulled up on me to pass. THAT woke me up and I came back to wakey wakey and stood on the thing, quickly pulling away from Chuck and eventually winning by a healthy margin in under two litre and was a solid seventh overall.

All concerned were stoked, especially Evey and the team mechanics that got a piece of the excellent prize money.

And as the points for over two litre and under two litre were exactly the same we left Augusta tied with the outright winner Dave MacDonald, a fantastic guy and great driver who tragically would lose his life at Indianapolis later that year. Not a good year for two great drivers so far.

Dave and I have our names etched into a permanent memorial at Augusta on the site of the race track; a friend, Henry T. Jones, keeps me posted about the place to this day (Facebook is great for reconnecting old friends, by the way). There is also a street named for Dave there. Fabulous.

So we motored back to Maryland with a bundle of cash from the prize pool and got set to go to Pensacola for the next USRRC event.

That one is another dim memory; I only know that we did not finish. I recall being quick there but I suppose something broke. These cars were not exactly super strong or reliable. That was the nature of Big Time Motor Racing at that point in time….

So we had a break until the next pro race, when Graham Shaw offered me his Cobra for the SCCA National Race at Marlboro in April. I naturally jumped at the chance. I also managed to sell my first ever money sponsorship, convincing a local Ford dealer to give us a few dollars in exchange for their name, "Tom & Martin Ford", on the front fenders in huge font. It couldn't have hurt that I had bought a new 1964 Thunderbird from them to drive to all the races that year. That was a wonderful, comfortable car to tour the USA in, I will tell you!

By the way Graham had a very odd nickname: everyone called him "Tombstone" Shaw. Strange for a racing driver and race car owner, hmmm? No clue where that one came from.

We qualified first; the Cobra would squirt down the short straights like a rocket propelled grenade and handled like a nimble snake on the twisty Marlboro corners. The oval was especially fun; I could drift the thing at about 80 and easily pick out a pretty face in the stands to wave to!

I won quite easily at Marlboro, whetting my appetite for the next USRRC event, scheduled for Riverside, California. Honest to God I fell in love with Southern California! The non-humid warm climate, the beaches, the fans – it was all great and I started thinking about why I stayed in humid old Wheaton, Maryland, really just a suburb of Washington DC, through muggy summers and bitter winters. But that is another tale for another time!

I loved the Riverside course too. I recall qualifying well and during the race found myself dicing with Ken Miles' Cobra, a rather daunting experience as Ken was as good as they get and the Cobra could have squashed my little Elva Porsche like a bug had Ken been that kind of driver, which he was not.

I have long since forgotten why we did not finish there however, as I have noted, the Elvas and other racing cars of that era were notoriously fragile. But I believe in this event it was an engine issue.

But next we would do Laguna Seca, which Evey and I had visited as spectators the year before to pick up the Super Genie Ford of Pedro Rodriguez for Bill McKelvey. I was really looking forward to that place with its hilly terrain and challenging fast turns one and two, near flat out for our ride.

Qualifying was easy again, and I took to the circuit as though it was my home race track! I flat loved that place (still do.) In the race we got a great 4th overall and first Under Two Litre. Joyous weekend!

Next up was Seattle's Kent raceway. This one was a terror as Bob Holbert, a friend from back East and a VERY good driver, crashed his Shelby King Cobra in the wet (it was ALWAYS wet in Seattle, seemed like). Bob narrowly missed us as he ended up crunching through the pits, destroying Skip Hudson's car and injuring himself (plus a little fire broke out), and badly injuring Nickey Chevrolet mechanic Ronnie Kaplan.

The signs at the time were all over the place: one can definitely get hurt or killed playing this game! But I ignored the signs steadfastly, or so it seemed. All these events would gradually eat away at my overconfident ego.... more later about that.

Again we scored a DNF. Failing to finish once again, especially at Kent which I really liked, had me muttering to myself despite Evey's best efforts at consolation. After all we badly needed the prize money from these events to keep going. But we did of course NOT think of quitting.

Honestly I do not recall exact times for many things in this book; it is turning out to be a lot harder to write than I expected it to be. Memories – some over 50 years ago – are less than clear and complete! And chronologies are uncertain. In any event I will keep going as long as health permits but hopefully you, the reader, will understand if some stuff seems sort of muddied. Moreover some of the stuff that happened makes me really mad – at ME. Young and dumber I suppose.

I shall overcome, I say!

Fast & Faster!

So now we headed back home to await the next race, at Watkins Glen New York, another circuit I fell in love with at first sight (most courses were new to me as I had only just become a full time pro road racer.) the Glen was famous as an originating venue for Sports Car racing, and also being the circuit where several US Grand Prix Formula One races were held.

I had been there to report on one Grand Prix race before for the Washington Daily News thanks to my friend, the reporter Ev Gardner. That was NOT fun; here I was around cars I knew I could go fast in and surrounded by people I knew I could run hard with. I did renew friendships there with such luminaries as Roger Penske, and (now Sir) Jackie Stewart whom I had met years before at Brands Hatch in England. But I digress.

The Elva Porsche had been overhauled since Kent, and was ready to rock and roll at the Glen; I easily qualified first in class and in the top five overall. Then in the race I ran off with it, finishing first under two litre and third overall. I had a lovely payday; the feeling of batches of Benjamins was really cool. Evey and I went back to Maryland, stopping at Manhattan Auto in Bethesda to brag!

Cash was now no longer an immediate problem either, which was a huge relief.

Next up was the race at Greenwood, in Iowa, in July, and this event would prove very auspicious for my future in racing. Carroll Shelby was there with both the GT production Cobras and the sports racing big cars, the King Cobras (British Coopers married to Ford V8 motors. The Chaparrals were there too. This was big time USRRC at its very best.

All these guys were fast. But I was damn well determined that wherever possible, I would be faster! I knew this season was like final exams for me to show my mettle and prove I had what it took to go all the way, to Indianapolis, to Formula One. I had big dreams and felt sure I was fast enough and that was that. Now was the time to show the racing world what I could do.

So I took to the rolling hills at Greenwood like the proverbial duck to water. This place was a bloody natural for me and I found I could outrun many of the "Big Cars" here. I qualified in the top four overall and way out front in the under two litre class. In the race I got a great start and darted up toward the front and found I could actually dice with Ed Leslie in his King Cobra! Carroll Shelby noticed and filed the information away for future use, which I discovered much later he would utilize, first in the fall, then again in 1965. But I am getting ahead of myself again here.

Fast & Faster!

Something failed on the car on the back side of the course so once again we were a DNF. Sad that. When I did not come around that lap, I heard later, Evey tried to run out on the track to find me and make sure I was okay, which I was. The team stopped her of course, but she was panicked. Hey y'all, we were definitely in LOVE big time. I still cherish my memories of that fine lady, my friends.

We had a nice break until the next USA race at Meadowdale Illinois, so I set up a deal with Carl Haas, and the British Racing Driver's Club, to race a factory Elva MK Vll with a BMW two litre power plant at Brands Hatch. The starting money would pay for Evey's and my trip to first Paris, then the French Riviera, then London.

I had pre-sold the car to a wealthy amateur racer in Washington DC so there was a nice profit and a grand trip to Europe for us in the deal. I got really sick in Juan les Pain, a beach resort near Nice. The doctor made a house call to our room, a proper French affair that came complete with a Bidet (took us an inquiry or three to find out what THAT thing was for).

The doc was really nice but spoke almost no English so communicating was a challenge as we had almost no French! But he said gently, Monsieur is avec malade. We could get that. Anyway he gave me some magic pills and I rested up listening to live Jazz from a concert on the lawn outside our window. Not a bad way to recover, that! In a day or two I was fine.

The beaches had NO sand; they were rock expanses lapped onto by the quiet Mediterranean Sea. But there was a fine French restaurant called Chez Nestou in a 500 year old olive oil mill! Sky high ceilings, huge vats and a large grove of olive trees out the back. We descended an endless staircase to get to the restaurant. It turned that monsieur Nestou was a magician as well as restaurateur, and he came to our table to perform, that made the whole trip for us (except of course for the racing!)

We were suitably entranced. What a trip this was turning out to be.

Finally Pan-Am-ing to London, we checked into a Hilton Hotel and immediately made our way to "Simpson's In The Strand" for their world renowned Prime Rib of Beef and Yorkshire Pudding. WOW. Unforgettable! (Evey later taught herself to make that meal and it was just as good. Great lady to say the least, many talents.)

Then it was off to Rye, driving the rent a car Hillman on the left side, which was unusual for a yank, of course. On the way we stopped for lunch at the New Inn, which was founded in 1580 or so! New indeed.... We were invited down to Frank Nichols' farm in Rye and a visit to the Elva works. Roy Vaness, a fine mechanic, had finished the setup on the Mark Vll and it sat there gleaming in the British fog.

Frank's farm was a site for raising hogs! Quite a contrast with racing cars, but I imagine building racing cars didn't produce sufficient income; racing in those days was far from lucrative. In any case Frank was as pleasant and courteous as could be and made us feel completely welcome in the UK.

It didn't hurt that by now the "malade" had cleared and I felt back to normal.

The next day was practice day for the Guards race at Brands; I hopped on board the Elva Mk Vll and promptly ran the damn thing off the road on the back side of the course in a fast right hand bend. I slid off into that grass and rammed the left side into a light standard sideways, bending the excrement out of the tubular chassis; good thing it was right hand drive mmm?

The crew, while taciturn, I am sure were thinking something like "damn stupid yank!" I sure as hell was! So the lads trundled off to the shops and amazingly made the car new overnight. Those blokes were bloody good, getting the car done on time so I could collect my absolutely crucial starting money (note that we had to actually start the race to collect.)

But the race was an unmitigated disaster. As I started at the green flag, the clutch went away and had a slipping tenuous engagement with the BMW engine! I limped around after the start and ended up completing just the one lap, enough for the payday but sure as hell a huge letdown after all the buildup all around. The yank did squat! What a trip!

I was really let down after Brands Hatch; although I had not expected to win outright or even come close, I had at least reckoned I could run in the top two or three in under two litre. One this that told me I would not win outright or two litre was watching a fellow flaunt a Brabham BT8 two litre car about like a champion dancer, shifting up on the straight so fast there must have been no more than a tenth of a second gap between gears!

His name? Denis Hulme, a future Can-Am star. Wow.

We got the Mk VII Elva sent to Baltimore and collected it in time to race, with the owner's blessing, at Mosport, then Watkins Glen, thanks to the generosity of car owner Brad Parker.

We DNF'd at Mosport, and then got a second at the Glen.

Next up was Meadowdale in the Elva Porsche.... THAT was a trip. A parabolic oval with a road course attached. My car LOVED that oval and ran fast right up at the top less than a foot from the guard rail, allowing me to qualify first under two litre (as was becoming a welcome habit).

In practice a weird accident happened: teammate Bob Markley went off at great speed and the Elva Porsche ended up right side up but twenty feet up in a tree! Carl Haas remarked that he was glad Markley wasn't hurt and what a shame it was the car was ruined. Then to me, sotto voce, said "sure is good for business though" with a slight grin. He was the seller of the cars to the team, which Oliver Schmidt dubbed "Scuderia Tin Can!" Droll wit that man had as did Carl....

We scored yet another Did Not Finish there; that was really getting old. We had a long string of DNFs interspersed with the occasional victory. Tough way to try to make a living.

Next up would come Mid-Ohio, a wonderful twisty fast course near Mansfield. I love this one too. A nice straight where we could hit 155 MPH in the Elva Porsche, followed up by a quick uphill chicane.

During the race, which I was leading at the time in under two litre, I lost it in the left turn part of the chicane, going straight off and creating a hill in the dirt, came down on the road in the right hander that the chicane led into, right in front of a shocked Joe Buzetta in a Porsche 904. Joe sought me out after the race and got all up in my face saying, "man you are crazy!" I smiled and said, "Yeah, don't forget it either" with a big scary grin. Joe never got in my way after that.

We had ended up seventh overall according to the fine website racingsportscars.com; I don't remember where in class but I want to remember we won under two litre again. (Grinning.)

Then came the Elkhart Lake 500 miler; Elkhart was a four mile circuit comprised of long straight and many 90 degree corners, and a sweeper called the Carousel, named after the turn at Nurburgring in Germany. That course perfectly suited the Elva Porsche and I was able to score seventh overall with one John Cannon, about whom there will be more said later in this chapter.

I want to say a word or two more about the team here. I regret that I do not remember their names because they were a great bunch of guys. No matter what happened with the car, they would get it ready for the next event. Not only that, they substituted the regular sort of vertical fan Porsche engine with a flat man, eventually going up to 1800 CCs. For a two litre car that thing had a lot of torque. Which came in very handy, especially on the twisty bits of the road courses we were running on.

After Elkhart Lake came Bridgehampton for me in a Shelby Cobra! Carroll Shelby did recognize that I could go quick at Greenwood, in the Elva Porsche, dicing with the much bigger and more powerful over two litre cars, and so he called me for the world championship race at Bridgehampton, New York to drive one of his superfast snakes. That was a scary course, with a downhill 120 MPH right-hand turn at the end of the pit straight!. That curve was slightly off-camber, on the outside of which was a gravel shoulder with no guard rail. Scary.

Especially in the cobra, which I stuck up out of like Wilt Chamberlin. Too tall I was at 6' 3" for this racing stuff. But that never stopped me, of course. I was hooked on the drug you can't buy.

We next went up to Canada to Mosport for a big pro race; another DNF. NOT a great season overall; it was very discouraging to me as I had hopes that this ride would pave the way for me to be sponsored in a big car. How mysterious the future can be…..

After Mosport was Riverside for the big pro race there. We are shown in the tabulations as did not appear but we did show up;

it was a flat fan Porsche engine failure that kept us off the grid, as I recall.

So then it was up to Monterey for the Laguna Seca pro event. This would turn out to be a lousy event for me thanks to a disgusting play by a teammate.

I was leading in the first of two 100 mile heats when I backed off to save the fragile engine and race car when I got taken out at turn nine, a 90 degree left hander, by my teammate John Cannon. What an asshat! Pulled it right in front of the team to boot.

We did not have team orders as such but common sense said Save The Cars. So much for that. I found it unforgivable, especially since I had recommended Cannon for the ride. Betrayal hurts.

When the second heat started I let Cannon go by, then on the fast left uphill going to the famous Corkscrew, there was a deep drop-off on the right, maybe 60 feet. I pulled up next to Cannon and pointed toward the drop letting him know two things: one, I was obviously quicker then he and two, if I wanted to put him off there he would have at least been badly hurt if not worse.

Unfortunately my engine gave up a bit later; I suspect it got revved a bit high when Cannon spun me out.

I don't recall where or if Cannon finished. But I damn well never spoke to that freak again!

Sometime around this time we bought a small but nice house in Wheaton, Maryland. We were able to assume a GI loan; the payment was less than $200 a month! Them was the daze!

So now it was on to 1965. We had no plans, no hopes; but we had our little house and each other. It was almost enough but not quite, sad to report.

Chapter 8: 1965

The Daytona 24 hour race was first on our calendar for 1965; I had no assigned car there but went anyway because, well, you just never know. I ended up with a Ferrari 250GTO, fast mother, I suspect it was actually a 275 engine, 3.3 litre instead of 3.0 litre. But I said nothing to no one! Driving at night, flat out on the back straight and flat at 180+ through the banked turn at the end of the straight, was a thrill I will never forget. My friend Bob Hurt drove too, as well as the car owner Peter Clarke. We were fast and reliable, ending up in 7th overall. I think we won a GT class too. Not bad for a pickup ride eh?

The record gets weird here because racingsportscars.com shows that I also raced a Mustang with Skip Scott there. Maybe I drove both; I do remember horsing the Mustang around but I was never comfortable in that car. I believe it was another DNF in any event.

Sebring, the classic 12 hour race, was next up for me as I recall. I had no ride there either but went down anyway with helmet bag firm in my grip. I hung out in Luigi Chinetti's NART pits just in case, when a torrential rainstorm arrived. The scheduled drivers would not drive the car as they reckoned it was way too dangerous, so Luigi told me to get in. the car, a Ferrari 275P2, had an open cockpit, and within a lap I had water up to my waist! Feet sloshing on the pedals, I kept it on the road and was actually having a blast, passing one car after another. In fact the only car that passed ME was the Ferrari 275LM Coupe of Walt Hansgen and Mark Donohue; they slipped past (I don't know which one was driving) on the straight behind the pits. I was amazed, those guys were really good.

I finished my stint as the rain abated and gave the car back to the other guys regretfully; I really enjoyed that ride and Chinetti was pleased that the car didn't sit pitside for an hour and a half! So I had a bit of a "fix" for my racing addiction there.

In late March I got one of THOSE awesome phone calls. It seemed that Carroll Shelby had recommended me to Craig Lang, a car owner who happened to be an heir to the Olympia (Washington) Brewery. There was funding and a car to drive, the "Lang Cooper". Was I interested?

You damn betcha!

Craig was the car owner for the late Dave MacDonald the year before, he and Wally Peat, the wrench man, were naturally devastated by Dave's untimely death. But being Racers with a capital R, it was gonna be onward and upward.

Fast & Faster!

Peter Brock, a well-respected car designer among his many other talents, had developed a beautiful body to shroud the Cooper Monaco chassis, and Craig and Wally got hold of a 364 cubic inch Traco Chevrolet built by THE guys to get "Strong Mother" engines from: Jim Travers (TRA) and partner Frank Coons (CO). That sweet engine made over 500 horsepower, a million pounds of torque to leap off corners, and was coupled to a robust Colotti gearbox, to complete the race car.

Leaving Evey at home I flew to Los Angeles to run some tests at Riverside with the Lang. I couldn't wait! Three months out of a car was more than I wanted to sit; I was itching to taste that freedom of going fast again. See, it was like I had this mind that ran on constantly, telling me what a jerk I was, that I would never be able to do anything right, that after all I was only human and shouldn't expect to be truly happy. Etc.

There were times when the mind was quiet, especially with my wife whom I loved deeply, but the rest of the time that silly sucker just chattered away. Getting into a race car shut the thing up after a couple-three laps! What peace there was at high speed. What ecstasy there was as in racing as I would OUTRUN the mind! Talk about something one HAD to have!

Addiction!

But back to business: I got off the big jet plane at LAX in a long wet day of never in sunny southern California RAIN, believe it or not!

I figured, maybe tomorrow it will be sunny as usual. Nope.

I had five days to get to see the Lang, to get to know the great Wally Peat as well as Craig, meet and observe the amazing Don Edmunds whose shop the car was in and who had built the sleek aluminum bodywork along with Wally, an expert welder who wielded a mean Heli-Arc!

And I knew that Craig Lang was the real deal when he took me to see his attorney in Los Angeles to sign off on an agreement not to sue Craig no matter what. Understood completely but I will swear here I NEVER would have sued Craig. He was a racer's racer!

Anyway. Five days of rain!

How lucky it is when you get to know a couple of great guys like Craig and Wally. We became friends almost instantly, which was a good thing, given that we were not going to be able to go to Riverside to practice. The rain never did let up.

But Craig and Wally took me to this great club in Santa Monica called The Ball. This was a topless joint that served a good lunch for a cheap price. I was inundated with swinging bare boobs for a couple of hours. Felt a little guilty to tell the truth!

I never did tell Evey about that one!

It was very interesting to me to see what happened at Pensacola, which I will write about shortly. Had what happened at Pensacola happened at Riverside it is extremely doubtful that I would be here talking about it. Anyway, I am getting ahead of myself again.

I cannot emphasize how gorgeous the Lang Cooper was. Peter Brock had done a magnificent job of designing, and Edmonds and his Anaheim shop had done an incredibly brilliant job of building the thing out of aluminum, and beaten into shape by Don and his experts' talented hands. And painted a glorious Red-Orange. I wish I could put pictures in this book.

So, I flew home to my darling wife, my little house, and settled down to wait. The first US Road Racing Championship event was at Pensacola, Florida, on an old airfield. I liked it. Even though there were no guard rails and not much runoff anywhere.

The main thing was, I finally had a car with enough horsepower to satisfy my need for speed!

I don't know exactly what the car weighed but I am guessing it was less than 1400 pounds. Even with a full tank and a 180 pound me on board, we probably had a power to weight ratio approaching three or four to one. That thing was quick and fast. Finally I had a car that I could get it on in big time.

The Lang Cooper was very satisfying to drive. Despite having had no practice in the car, it felt absolutely right to me and I had no problems sorting the car out so it worked for my style, and getting it pointed in the right direction. I loved how that thing would flat scat off corners.

We were fast right off the transporter, and I was blowing off a lot of guys that I not really expected to beat, not so soon. People like Walt Hansgen, for example.

Then the excrement hit the rotating device, big time. I was accelerating at somewhere around 120 MPH on the straightaway in front of the pits, when something broke in the right rear suspension. The car turned right all by itself. I found myself ducking down as the car headed right into the pit area where it ended up crumpled on top of hay bales that were trying to catch fire. I had absolutely no control.

I even ran through the starter's flag station and mauled Jesse Coleman's set of flags badly. Later he sent me the mechanical black flag with a note in the orange center saying "you missed me!"

But literally the car, which it developed later, had a disastrous propensity to make unnatural and unexpected right turns, could well have killed him. And me. I pretty much ignored such possibilities, but little by little these things ate into my confidence....

So Wally and Craig trundled the car up onto its transporter and headed back to California to do an awful lot of work. The gorgeous red orange paint job was history. The car's next appearance would be in bare aluminum.

Riverside is next. I LOVE Riverside. Can't wait!

But first we have to get there. I had a jillion miles on the 64 T-bird so we sold it in 1964 and tried a Mustang. Hated it! Sold that in Las Vegas and flew home to buy a nice used Cadillac convertible. Great ride for a cross country trip. Nice reliable transportation, right?

Wrong.

We left way early for the West Coast so as to enjoy a leisurely trip, seeing the sights and relaxing in nice motels each night after a good meal. This worked out just fine. Until Arizona.

Fast & Faster!

There is a nice little desert hamlet on the southern route through Arizona called Gila Bend. Maybe 1500 people in those days. Plus a big truck stop. It's in a valley surrounded by sandy hills with sagebrush and mesquite abounding. Climbing the slope out of Gila Bend, all at once out of nowhere the water temperature shot up and that stinky smell of boiling coolant took over for the sights and sounds. The damn car was broken!

We limped back down the hill to the truck stop where we met a mechanic, and owner of the truck stop, by the name of Andy Anderson. Andy allowed as how it was a water pump gone south and informed us that he would have to get a new one sent in and it would not be there until the next day so we should check in to the one motel in town (which was actually quite decent.) We were not concerned about getting to Riverside as this was only Tuesday and we had until Friday morning to arrive for practice for the USRRC race there.

So into the motel we ensconced and set up our camp at the clean, invigorating pool. Evey and I talked, made love, played gin rummy and generally just kicked way back awaiting the Cadillac repairs to be made, we thought, the next day.

Wrong again. Around noon Wednesday we paid the bill, checked out of our motel and hit the road again. Made it out of town, air conditioning humming, and halfway up the damn hill guess what? Same shit different day. Water temp off scale. Boiling coolant. Whiskey Tango Foxtrot?!

Back down the hill, pulling into the truck stop. Pissed but not rude to Andy, explained damn car not repeat not fixed and would he please get it done so we could continue to motor to Riverside where I had a race to run. He said of course he would and had no idea why it did not work as he had put a new water pump in. Etc.

Back to the motel, check in again, get out the cards. Did I mention it was like a Sauna in Gila Bend? Over a hundred degrees in the shade. HOT like I had never experienced. But Evey loved it and as I got used to it I found it was live-with-able as there was zero humidity, the thing that made Washington D.C. summers so miserable.

Another day and night goes by and we are back at Anderson's at noon the next day. Thursday. Plenty of time to make it to the race track. No sweat, right?

Wrong.

Relieved and rested, we take off up the hill.

NO! The god cursed Cadillac did the sane act! Water temperature off scale. Stinky boiling coolant. Back down the hill. Back to a shocked and distraught Andy. This time we started to get really worried but Anderson assured us he would figure it out. Okay, back to the motel, cards out, gin rummy played in sweltering heat interspersed with dips in the cool pool. Not trusting that Anderson could fix the car but what choice did we have? He was the only mechanic in this desert so called oasis.

Back to his shop Friday morning. We would JUST make it in time for a night's sleep if we left by noon.

Up the hill. And guess what? Same thing three days in a row? Yep.

This time I got out of the car, cussed up a blue streak while Evey held her hands to her ears, then delivered a huge kick to the driver's side door panel, denting it in about half a foot.

Limped back down and accosted Andy. NOT FIXED AGAIN we politely shouted. He was as shocked as we were but said he would get right on it, dropping everything else. I explained we needed to have been outta there by noon that day to make it to Riverside at a decent hour to rest up before Saturday morning practice and qualifying.

So at this point we had to charter an airplane to fly us to Riverside Friday night! That wreaked some havoc on the budget, that I can assure you of! But we got there, rented a car,

Fast & Faster!

got a fitful night's sleep and next day, Saturday morning, we set out to practice.

The car was in bare aluminum this time; the bodywork had been pounded out but there was no time to repaint the thing. And ever witty Craig had painted happy feet on the back with the legend "Made in Peyton Place, Piece by Piece" above. Jim Hall's wife Sandy, on spying this legend, muttered angrily "racing doesn't need that stuff" and smoldered off, leaving me with a sense that Craig had a sense of humor but Sandy? Well, Sandy was Sandy! A real lady. God bless her.

The Lang was as fast if not faster at Riverside than Pensacola. The sweeping esses were where the car really shone; clipping the inside of turns a bit past the apex and standing on the gas so it leapt like a cat to the next corner. Coming up the hill into turn six John Cooper's chassis did the job brilliantly, thanks to Craig Lang, Wally Peat and Peter Brock's hard work to avoid either understeer ("Push") or oversteer ("Looseness"). It was as close to being neutral as was possible with this rapid a racing car. The driving of the car was an utter joy!

Note: The chassis was new for 1965, a replacement for the one wrecked in the rain by Bob Holbert in fall 1964 at Kent.... see the chapter on 1964 for the sad details. At least Holbert was only hurt, and no one was killed. Though it was sure close.

Of course when you bolt a 500 plus horsepower engine into a chassis originally designed for a 2.7 litre Coventry Climax engine that on a good day probably made 280 horses, you are gonna have issues, as we had at Pensacola.

But then, who cared. The car was so fast out of the tight turn seven that emptied onto the back straight it pinned me back against the firewall. VERY satisfying, that!

Into the final corner, turn nine, a semi-banked long sweeper, that thing stuck like glue and going onto the pit straight into turn one was trippy! One was a very fast left-bending affair of at least 110 MPH that you just clipped the apex in, steering mostly with the gas pedal. I loved it!

We had run some fast laps in practice and I was relaxing when I heard myself get paged to come to pit entry. What a shock! There waiting to get let in is the mechanic who had come all the way from Gila Bend, Arizona! It was our new friend Andy Anderson, with the Cadillac, all fixed and running like new.

Albeit with that gimongous dent in the driver's door: some nitwit asked me what had happened to that door. I just replied, "It seemed like a good idea at the time", and hopped in to drive to our pit with a beaming Andy in the shotgun chair.

The guy had taken it on himself to drive the car out from Gila Bend and deliver it in person. What a guy! I got Andy a pit pass and a sticker for the car and we celebrated the reunion with hot dogs and cokes in the summery sun. Wow.

Besides Andy and of course Craig and Wally and their bosom bud Joe Freitas, Peter Fonda, whom we had met in Nassau last winter, is also in our pits. Nicest guy you could imagine. Not a star. Just a friend. He would play a pivotal role a bit later that weekend....

Race Day: A bright, sunny, warm SoCal weather welcomed us and we were ready willing and able to make going fast and faster happen. I was convinced that, after a good qualifying, I could win this sucker outright and I bloody well intended to.

Before the race I took my usual 20 minutes to sit quietly in the Caddy and just rest the body and mind. No interruptions allowed please. And then I am ready to dance at 180 MPH!

When the green flag dropped I got a great start off the line and leapt into a fair lead; the Lang was working beautifully. I was stoked to be in front of Hall in the Chaparral, Wester in a fast Genie and Sharp in the other Chaparral.

The Lang was fast and smooth as I wended my way through the esses into six, then darting down to seven and seven-A the engine sang with that throaty roar that only a well tweaked V8 can produce. I left the field behind for about six laps before the car showed its fragile nature once again.

It was a real moment, over which I should not have gotten because I really should have been real badly hurt or killed and probably killed a dozen or so spectators as well.

I am the car. I am the turning. The shining asphalt. I am the guard rail, the spectators, the blazing sunlight. I am the crisp bite of Firestones on the road. I am all of it.

Then I point the car into turn one at probably 120 MPH. the car decides to turn right instead of left! I have zero control; the car lurches sideways up the sandy embankment toward a gaggle of spectators behind a snow fence. (Flashes back to Sebring 63!)

Oh God! People are going to get hurt. Killed.

But somehow the people are missed as the racer careens down the road sliding, I smell gasoline, the fuel tank has torn open.

I end up waaayyyy down the racetrack, in turn four. Finally the car stops. I have been standing on the brake pedal all the way and trying to steer but the rack and pinion steering has broken away from the frame!

I am stopped and stunned but unhurt. Alive. Okay.

Fast & Faster!

Fellow racer Ronnie Bucknum has a motorcycle and offers me a ride to the pits. I thank him and climb aboard.

It is all surreal.

Peter Fonda had been watching the race near turn one. He ran back when he saw the crash, shouted to Evey, "Charlie crashed and boy is he pissed!" Brilliant. In that instant Evey knew I was all right, unhurt and naturally angry as hell.

I have as the saying goes, dodged a large bullet. Again. Twice in a row the car has turned right unbidden by the driver. I am a passenger only at these times. Scary? Hell yeah. But I stuff it down and accept a hug from Evey and warm wishes from Wally, Craig, Andy, Joe.

So that is that. We bundle it all up and Evey and I head to the airport with Andy to get him transported back to Arizona.

I am reeling inside while pretending to be calm outside but refuse to really accept that this one ought to have at least hurt the body real bad….

Evey and I drove up to Laguna Seca for the next race as the crew took the car back to Don Edmunds' shop to get rebuilt again. And why Craig – and I – didn't call it quits right then I will never know. I did reflect on the possibility, very real, that had the steering rack broken away in private testing at

Riverside the outcome would have been, well, drastically worse.

But that is racing. The drug you cannot buy.

The record indicates we came in 8th at the next race at Laguna Seca but honestly I do not remember racing there at all. And we would miss the next USRRC round, at Bridgehampton as the car needed massive attention. But Craig and Wally turned up for the Mosport Players 200 in June, and we were ready to go after that bit of a layoff.

The car was back in full bloom, its red-orange livery gleaming and everything in good order. I had practiced braking my Caddy with my left foot across country as I figured one advantage Jim Hall had with his fast self-designed Chaparral was the automatic transmission he had, which allowed him to brake with the left foot, saving tenths of seconds each time. I wanted to do that and the Colotti gearbox didn't mind being shifted sans clutch. So we were set up to do well at Mosport against some significant competition, the fastest of which was World Champion John Surtees in a very rapid Lola- Chevrolet.

Qualifying could not have gone better. The left foot braking worked like a charm and we set a time quite close to Surtees in the red rocket. I loved Mosport with its twisty bits, fast up and

Fast & Faster!

downhill corners, a good long straight and man that place tested me. Great fun!

The Players race was in two 100 mile heats. We managed a respectable sixth overall for the two, but where we really showed what we could do was in heat #2, where I ran second, beaten only by John Surtees (no shame in being whipped by a World Champ, you know.) About 20 miles from the end the battery, which was in the cockpit, came adrift and was flung about tethered by the cables! It splashed battery acid on my face (remember no full face helmets back then) but I just felt a wet sensation. No pain. But then the moment the checkered flag dropped, my face was on fire!

I hustled into the pits and yelled water! Pointing to my face. It took a bit to get the point across. Man that was sensational discomfort.

Craig and Wally seemed to be pleased with the result but I also knew that the many mechanical glitches were wearing on all of us, especially Craig, but we would solider on for a while. We headed to Maryland in caravan and holed up at Evey's and my house in Wheaton. We passed the time partying while waiting for Watkins Glen which was coming up next.

Fast & Faster!

The car looked fabulous in its red-orange livery; drew a lot of attention wherever it was parked on its slant bed transporter.

That remind me: On the road, Craig and Wally had this two sided sign and when they spied a foxy lady driving along they would flash it: One side said "HI!" And the other said "Coffee?" Rumor had it that there were plenty of coffee breaks driving across country. The transporter was a self-contained six wheeled affair with that slanted bed for the race car, racks for wheels and lots of cabinets built in for tools, spares and luggage. Really neat!

Wally and his stewardess (oops, flight attendant) girlfriend found a hideaway and Craig stayed with us; we imported a lady friend of Evey's to keep him company. There were no complaints heard anywhere. Good times.

I had a little Honda motorcycle and we rode it up and down the hilly back yard for fun. Drinks on the patio!

Watkins Glen was another favorite course; I loved the long straight stretches and swooping fast turns. I had won there with the Elva Porsche so I was eager to get back there. Unfortunately the car did its right turn number yet again as something broke in the first part of the chicane. This was too much especially for Craig. He swapped the car, minus engine, to Skip Scott, a Philadelphia area racer, for a lovely Ferrari Lusso 250GT. Couldn't blame the guy; he had put up with a lot from that whole half season!

Evey and I discussed the scene and decided to avail ourselves of a new McLaren M1A from Carl Haas. We had just enough money left from inheritances and sale of the Elva Porsche but I was worried about money to run the car. We needed sponsorship. I was reluctant to do so but Evey insisted I call Nickey Chevrolet in Chicago as we knew their car had been destroyed by the Bob Holbert King Cobra crash at Kent in the fall.

So Evey prevailed and I called Al Seelig, Nickey's race team guy. I think I said, "You wouldn't want to sponsor my McLaren for the fall pro races wouldja?" Hard sell! I about fell over when he said yes and voila! We were set for the fall season car and money wise.

In those days it was rare indeed to be able to make money in road racing. Most of the drivers had money or made a good living outside of racing and so could pay their own bills.

Very few made it as a team that was self-sufficient, like Mark Donohue and Roger Penske did. Roger was a dynamite businessman and sponsor-getter; still is fifty years later.

Fast & Faster!

Back to the season: Craig agreed we could use his two engines; how awesome was that! Wally stayed on and the four of us made our way to Anaheim to Don Edmunds' shop to set the new car up. We got the car quick, picking it up in early August at LAX. Wally and Craig installed the 364 CID engine; the car came with a new but strong Hewland 4 speed LG500 gearbox (Mike Hewland was a witty one, LG meant – what else – Large Gearbox!) and Chevy bell housing. We were happy as hell to have a car that might go where pointed instead of making all those disastrous right turns!

The first event for the McLaren was to be Continental Divide Raceway south of Denver. Neat road course that. Practice with the McLaren went really well, until….

Uh oh.

Wally didn't trust the small Varley battery that came in the car and there was no place to put a bigger one, so he installed an alternator! Unheard of in a Group Seven/USRRC car, but hey he was the wrench so I said nothing. Big mistake on both our parts.

Look: Varley's were used in Formula One, Sports racing cars, and all other sorts of racing cars. No problem even in 500 mile races as far as I knew. Well, shit:

We had aerospace quality braided steel hoses everywhere replacing the junky rubber hoses. Braided steel hose was milspec standard, so we naturally went for it. All good, right?

But as I was running flat out on a straight the damn car burst into flames. I had just motored by a flag station wherein there were fire extinguishers and was going way too fast to get the car whoa'd for that one and the next one was at the end of the straight. So I made a rapid choice to go on to that place and if I got burned so be it, but I was flat NOT going to lose the car, I had way too much invested in that sled. Fortunately I made it.

Obviously.

What had happened is the damn alternator had "arced" a pinhole in an oil hose, and oil got squirted onto the headers. Boom. Instant bonfire.

I suppose one could say I was royally pissed. I didn't get too much up in Wally's face though. Friend as well as mechanic. Shit happens in racing like everywhere else except more so in this game!

So that ended our weekend but the racing gods felt bad about it I guess because as I was sipping a cold one in the bar that evening a cool guy named Ted Lobinger from Goodyear approached me and said he would pay me a LOT of money to

Fast & Faster!

switch from Firestones to Goodyears. The racing rubber was just as good and the bucks were great. Huge help. I had a burnt (somewhat) racing car and no prize money would be had on this weekend so quite naturally I jumped on that in a Split Nano Second! Ted and I also became friends in the process so that was neat too.

So it was back to Don's shop in Anaheim and lotsa work to get ready for Mid-Ohio, about 2500 miles away. Busy doesn't begin to describe it.

I have said it before: I LOVED Mid-Ohio. One of the most fun, must drive hard, road courses ever. But I don't remember a thing about the race. I believe Hap Sharp won in a Chaparral and according to the record I came second. Not too bad for the car's first actual race. I felt the investment was going to work out. Wally and Craig had stayed on board and somehow as I mentioned I ended up with the two 364 CID engines and a set of 58MM Side Draft Weber carbs which were far better than the standard issue 48MM Down drafts.

Next up was the first of the fall Pro races, at Ste. Jovite in Canada. We didn't run well and didn't finish there. There was some dissension in the team also; I don't recall details but something had gone off. I remember it rained and I hated that track in the wet. Too much fast off camber no guard rails etc.

Anyway, next was Mosport. We qualified 7th among a large international field and ended up finishing fourth. Not all that bad but the team was falling apart. Somewhere around here Wally and I had to agree to disagree. Might have been that alternator thing or some other issue.

Overall I would say that it was probably more me than Wally. Peat was a fine mechanic and good man, and I had a hard time getting along with people, always had! I was always a bit of a loner. And somewhat, well maybe more than somewhat, arrogant!

I still consider Wally a friend but there was something about the way we were that didn't work for me, so when I got back to the West Coast I hired mechanic/engineer Bruce Burness, the ex USRRC Championship winner with George Follmer. Bruce was VERY talented so he didn't come cheap; nevertheless he was a necessary addition. Nice guy too.

And like Wally, a former Shelby mechanic. And, I later read that at some point Craig Lang said it just wasn't fun for him anymore. There went some key support!

I felt confident we could compete at the next race, a Pro race at Kent, near Seattle, Washington. The car felt solid and went where I pointed it, but still lacked some cornering speed compared to the works McLarens of Bruce himself and Phil Hill, and the Chaparrals. Kent had nifty uphill sections, a fast straight and a fast as hell corner that led onto that straight. That turn had Holbert spin into the pits in the wet the previous year. Ironically that was sort of the start of how I ended up with the Nickey Chevrolet sponsorship.

Kent also ran counter-clockwise which I had always liked as my home road course, Marlboro, Maryland, was counter-clockwise too, having been an add-on to a short track oval.

Bruce Burness, his assistant Terry and I were finishing car prep of the McLaren M1B at Kent when a young lad came by to see if he could join us. Of course, we said. As we worked away he mentioned he had some engineering ideas. He had driven up in one of those Volvo sedans that looked for all the world like a '41 Ford, and poking through the roof was a solid rod with a wing attached. Weird! But as he talked we figured that while slightly odd he was brilliant and we listened.

His name? Trevor Harris.

Later to be of Shadow Can-Am fame with Don Nichols, about whom more later.

He pointed out that the rear suspension would create a lot of bump camber change, i.e. when the wheels went up the very wide tires would tilt in and lose a whole lot of their contact with the ground. A simple upward move of the inboard mounting point for the upper rear suspension link would flatten out the camber and create better tire contact, especially in corners and on accelerating out of said corners!

Of course this would make the car want to roll more (the arcane bit of data called the roll center would move down a bunch) so a very big anti-roll bar was also in order. How Bruce got all that done at Kent is a mystery, in fact since my memories are far from reliable it is more likely that it all got done in the shop before the next event at Laguna Seca in Monterey, California.

I do know that the car felt really quick in practice and qualifying, with one little incident that could have been a huge disaster. In those days my driving shoes were a pair of Italian loafers from Lefcourt of Lexington and 47th in New York city. Why? They were really comfortable.

I would strap them on with duct tape (AK Racer's Tape) and they worked fine. Except one time when the right one came halfway off i9n the middle of braking for a 75 MPH left hander! That was a wild thrash, let me tell you. But I made it back to the pits and retaped it. All fine after that. Sheesh. Racing!

Fast & Faster!

I don't recall a lot about the race there at Kent except that I was able to dice with World Champion Phil Hill in a works McLaren – quite fun, that was – and I ended up a respectable fourth behind the two factory McLarens of Phil and Bruce, and a Chaparral (Hap Sharp, I think,)

Trevor came to Laguna Seca with us and helped again with a huge transparent spoiler to get the back end to stick, as the downforce was minimal with the stock M1A bodywork. On the back Trevor penned a note to Hall: hey Jim, it's a solar cell! Genius and sense of humor. One of my favorite people ever....

With that spoiler, about a foot tall, I could literally toss the car sideways and stand on the gas steering and sliding sideways playing with the throttle, in turn nine for example, and accelerate with impunity!

That thing was like a Go kart with the suspension changes, big anti-roll bars and that demon VERY effective spoiler.

Trevor and Bruce had transformed that car.

Laguna was a favorite course: turn two, a sweeper that I could just power drift slightly at maybe 120, the fabulous turn up the hill with a drop off to the outside that could be scary if I thought about it (I didn't) toward the corkscrew. A rollercoaster, that one, cresting a steep hill with a hard left, swooping down to turns 7 and 8, fast right hand sweepers leading into hard braking for turn nine, my favorite turn nine; getting that right gave us a whole lot of straightaway speed. Tight, fast, fun!

In our time sheets we set fastest time and won pole except the officials had a different set of times! Annoying as hell; we were sure we had pole. But officialdom won as they pretty near always do!

Anyway, we got a good start and ran up front but I honestly don't remember where. I do know the engine was running hot; I slowed to save it. I think we ran about last for the two heats as it turned out.

One part of 1965 was great fun: Dan Blocker, "Hoss" on TV's Bonanza, was doing promo work for Nickey. We met and became friends, and he was, via Nickey, associated with our race car. Neat guy! He was at Laguna and a number of other races and was very supportive.

He and Evey got to be friends and Blocker invited her to the tapings of Bonanza. She accepted at once; beat the hell out of sitting around while the crew and I worked on the race car. To tell the truth I think she had a crush on actor Michael Landon; she sure talked about him a lot. But no harm no foul there!

Back to the Laguna Seca race: One minor glitch happened in the second heat (there were two 100 milers). In the left hander going up the hill I was either leading or second, when the engine overheated big time, water and oil temperatures off scale, and suddenly the water header tank burst, dumping a ton of water on the right rear tire.

The car flew sideways and seemed to float in midair. I remember a thought going by on a scrolling ticker tape like those signs in New York. It said, "I wonder how long I'll be in the hospital?"

The car landed hard, in a cloud of dust and steam. A flagman ran toward me with a giant fire extinguisher and shouted, "What happened"? I said, "What do you think happened? I shit my pants!" He fell down laughing.

All that happened to the car is the shock absorbers were deflated; all the rest including me were okay.

I walked back to the pit entry, a long stroll through spectator areas, and at the gate, I started through, face dirty around where goggles were not, in my Goodyear uniform, carrying my helmet, when the wanker at the gate said, "where's your pit pass?" I damn near knocked him over as I strode through.

Fast & Faster!

Surprisingly I was pleased despite the disastrous day: I had shown, in my own view that I could race with the best. These events had Indy car stars, formula one drivers, a world champ or two or three, and so on. Guys like Graham Hill, Jimmy Clark, Parnelli Jones, Phil Hill, Bobby Unser, Roger Penske, Jim Hall, Mark Donohue, Lothar Motschenbacher, Dan Gurney, Bob Bondurant, Ken Miles and on and on. And I had run up with them!

It was like, yes. I CAN do this and I can do this well. A real boost to my confidence as a racing driver!

Next was the LA Times GP at Riverside, Qualifying mid pack was as much as we could realistically expect so I was okay with that because here I was racing with the best in the world, most of the same people that were at Laguna Seca the week before.

The car was great on the turns but lacking top speed; I got passed by Jimmy Clark to lose third in the race as he steamed by going into turn nine in his piece of crap Lotus 40!

Only Clark could have brought that awful thing in third in a huge international field of superstars.

Fast & Faster!

But a fourth place was satisfying given the field. And we had a couple of races to go; Las Vegas, then our winter holiday in Nassau, Bahamas.

I didn't realize at the time what an enviable life I was leading!

In Vegas we ran really well until, while fourth, a fitting that held the line that went to the oil pressure gauge blew out and so that was that. One of the mechanics had used an A.N. fitting in a pipe thread aperture. Dumb mistake. Of course all the mistakes were basically unsmart!

Big disappointment as I felt good about scoring another fourth in a big field of pro drivers. But that, my friends, is racing! As I may have said before!

And Nassau was a bit of a bust, apart from the seven days of parties and the free rooms at the Nassau Beach Lodge, of course…. I don't recall what happened in the feature but I know it wasn't good. But we did win one event.

And I got to play my Alto Saxophone at one of the parties. Blew a few bars of modern jazz.

Then on checkout, I got a $700 phone bill at the Nassau Beach Lodge. One of our crew had a girlfriend he was phone-loving in California, it seemed. I put it on my American Express. Uncomfortable off-pissing moment, that.

Fast & Faster!

As it turned out we would sell the car in January so it all came right financially in the end. And we would find money in other ways as well. But man that phone bill did hurt!

We were shown as 46th in the Sunday Nassau feature! Not what we envisioned especially since we had won that short race called the Nassau Classic.

Chastened by Nassau's lousy feature result, Evey and I went back to Maryland and landed in 12 inches of snow after the bliss of sunny Nassau. Culture shock!

Around this time I had a future inheritance that I borrowed on from a relative. Then I ran low again and borrowed using the same collateral, from another party. Eventually that meant the relative did not get repaid. I felt and still feel great regret about those actions. Racing. The drug you CAN buy. I would do about anything to be able to go pro racing. There have been guys who ended up in jail for doing stuff to go racing that the law frowned upon!

To paraphrase the late great Tenor Saxophone master Stan Getz, racing was my life, at the expense of everything else in my life.

We had acquired a new Chevrolet Caprice at wholesale from Nickey; that car was a slug despite the 396 CID engine. I had road tested Al Seelig's car; I came to believe strongly that there were undisclosed hop-ups in that thing. Nickey DID have a speed shop after all. And Al ran the thing, of course, along with anything competition oriented.

A last hurrah for the M1A was the annual freeze fest in early January, at Marlboro, the "Refrigerator Bowl" regional. We took the McLaren there to do an exhibition run and obliterated the lap record, of course. NOT difficult for the fabulous McLaren Group Seven ride!

Most fun a guy could have with his clothes on.

Chapter 9: 1966

Having had a fair showing in 1965 with the McLaren M1A, I was very confident that for 1966 we could run with the big dogs, so with fresh Nickey Chevrolet sponsorship we acquired a new McLaren M1B from old pal Carl Haas, then the Elva and McLaren importer. Carl was fun to deal with and negotiate prices with; he gave us a good deal so no complaints on that score ever.

(A silly note: Some called this McLaren a Mark II and the 1965 car a Mark I. Others used the M1A and M1B name. I've used the latter.... just because!)

Traco was building 333 CID engines for '66 and we got two so as to hopefully have a backup as needed. These engines were not as powerful as the 364 CID engines we had run in 1965 but supposedly would last longer. I knew better that to argue with Jim Travers, or partner Frank Coons. These guys were THE engine builders to use; builders of the trademarked "Strong Mothers". They were IT unless we built or own; only one guy I knew of to do that was the inimitable Chuck Parsons, a renaissance man of motor racing if there ever was one. There were doubtless others I didn't know.... Chuck and his bride Sherry were really good people and they are missed sorely. Anyway....

Fast & Faster!

We had a commitment to Goodyear for a tire test session at Riverside, which would go 3-4 days. The test was great with two exceptions: we put an awful lot of miles on the car. And too many on the essential ring & pinion in the Hewland box of gears. Of course the upside was that we had the car really dialed in at Riverside

And I ran off and damaged the body work during a rain tire test where the guys had wet down the course....

I ditched it, plowing off into a sandy berm which buggered the beautiful Paul Knierim artwork he had painstakingly done at Edmunds' shop. Ooh God. We had a big showing scheduled for the Newporter Inn in Newport Beach. Press from all over showed up, Carl Haas came out from Chicago, and Goodyear brought their team headed up by my friend Ted Lobinger.

Everyone was really stoked with the car which looked great thanks to the painter whose, I'm sorry, first name escapes me now. I remember his last name, Wilson. Maybe Burrell? He and striper and artist Paul Knierim patched it up very well, they did.

As we said in SoCal at that time, it looked "Bitchin".

At the showing in Newport Beach, Road & Track immediately asked if they could put the car on the cover. That was an easy yes; think about the exposure for the sponsors. So we rolled the car outside in the sunny parking lot and the photographer borrowed a stepladder from the Inn, and took about a million pictures, one of which ended up on the cover of the July 1966 issue. If you look very closely you can just see Paul's tape patchwork on the nose of the car.

Then they asked us to let them do a road test of the car; this, they said would be the fastest car they ever tested. Duh, yes of course, much sponsor joy involved. We had, besides Nickey and Goodyear, Valvoline, Wiggins Aerospace connectors, Lamson & Sessions Grade Eight hardware, Airheart Disc Brakes, Aeroquip braided steel hoses, K & B model cars and more. Crew Chief Ed Schafer was in large measure responsible for getting all that great California product sponsorship; he had been a busy boy.

And we made them all happy as clams at this stage of the season!

After a lucrative tire test for Goodyear, and a couple of days to get ready after the R&T test, we went off to Las Vegas for the first round of the USRRC with high confidence. We should have known better. After a sane practice and qualifyingsession, I believe we had the pole or maybe Jerry Grant did, it was close. We started the race dicing with Jerry in the Lola, but shortly after I was right on Grant's tail when he went off onto the gravel shoulder and sprayed my front end with rocks and gravel. It was like shrapnel; busted the radiator open and that was our race. Disgusting, that was.

I was pissed but what could we do. How many times did we say, "That's racing."

For Riverside the following weekend we were pressed for time because of all the work needed after Vegas, and arrived late on Saturday where Jerry Grant was already getting the award for a pole position qualifying lap. We were a bit annoyed, but he was much more so when I rolled off the trailer and summarily eclipsed his time, setting a new lap record. Man, Jerry was shocked.

All that time tire testing really paid off.... at least at first.

A half hour or so before the race is to start I find myself unwilling to be with people....

I cannot engage in idle chatter.... I must sit quietly and alone in my road car, windows up, doors locked, engine humming softly, air conditioning creating coolness and white sound. I sit. I Am. There is nothing. I am that nothing. At Peace for now ...

No mind, at the 'time' it is - just Being.

Fast & Faster!

I come out and hear sounds, the announcer talking, engines being started and vroom vroom as the mechanics clear the engine's throats then mostly silence as the race cars are wheeled out to the starting line for the standing start of the event near Los Angeles.

There is stillness, perfect silence. I Am that.

Then it is time to go.

I rub my face, stretch, grab my helmet and stroll out to the grid. So many people. Brightly painted racecars decorated with myriad sponsor's messages. The crowd a blur, humming, murmuring, anticipating wild excitement.... eager. I step into the car. The crew helps me strap in. Everything is calm and yet there is anticipation. So soon there will be frenetic action, sound and fury. I put in earplugs, work my head into the helmet, and sit. Waiting peacefully. Heart rate normal. Breath steady.

The grid is cleared of all except the cars and the drivers. An official announces, "Gentlemen, start your engines." (No ladies in this race, today....)

I flip off the aircraft safety cover and flick a switch up. The system is armed. Another safety cover up, and a spring-loaded

Fast & Faster!

toggle is nudged up and the start whirs, the engine coughs, sputs, fires. Rummm Rummm Rumm BLAT. Brraap. Braap.

Plugs cleared, the right foot relaxes and sets at a steady fast idle, 1500 RPM. I wait and watch. Not Knowing. The inner trembling begins, like a precursor to orgasm. Energy roams the body and tries to trigger the mind to label the experiencing as fear and add, "I am afraid" but it cannot.

The mind is in abeyance. It rests in, as, the instant. There is No time. Just Now.

The green flag drops. Rear wheels spinning furiously grabbing the tarmac, the car-driver complex launches itself toward turn one. In the lead. Through turn two flat out.

Sweeping into three, just light braking then standing on it through four, bending left and braking through five into the off-camber decreasing radius six, a favorite.

Accelerating down a slope into the cresting hill leading into seven. Through 7a onto the straight.

180 MPH into nine, a long sweeper, powering through in a slight controlled drift! Past the pits, a wave to Bruce and Evey. Through turn one again, drifting and accelerating....

Everything becomes nothing, and nothing becomes everything.

Fast & Faster!

There Is Just…. The Racing.

I had warned Grant before the start that we had just put in new brake pads and might not be able to stop as good as usual and please don't run over me.

It was true but me and the car just flat out took off and I left Grant struggling along behind as I jumped into a solid lead. The lead I would never relinquish until….

The first thing that happened is that about halfway through the race, I damn near got overwhelmed by the intense heat of the desert and a hot race car. No drink bottle on board!

I was starting to get afraid of passing out when, probably blessedly, the ring and pinion in the Hewland gearbox wore itself out. All that testing, plus without my knowledge Ed Schafer, our lead mechanic, had "run in" the gearbox on a lathe before we turned a wheel. Ah well, I am sure to Ed it seemed like a good idea at the time. I probably would have vetoed it. Straight cut gears don't need "running in".

Anyway, that was a brutal disappointment, having a nearly insurmountable lead, and then losing…. again. Two miserable races in a row.

Helluva way to start what was supposed to be my best season yet, eh?

Having less than a week to get ready for the next race at Laguna Seca meant near panicky phone calls to Mike Hewland to acquire a new Ring and Pinion. In the process we discovered that the early LG500 boxes used a modified Jaguar ring and pinion (in British, Crown Wheel & Pinion) a weak point for sure. But Mike was no slouch; he had made his own, a lot stronger. In fact that new one lasted almost all year. One replacement for wear as I recall. Pretty darn good that.

By the way: Some when around here I was named by a writer named Dennis Cipnic in Autoweek as one of the top ten racing drivers in the world. Wow. I guess there was some talent in addition to money buried in there somewhere!

We arrived at Laguna Seca with the McLaren in good working order and the driver well hydrated! After a good qualifying session where we won the pole, I figured I was ready to finally win one. But I bungled the start.

On the line; when the green flag dropped I found myself with a box full of neutrals. A whole bunch of cars streamed past me as I fished around for first. I finally got going.

I'm steamed. Screwed that start. Stupid. Sheesh. But the car is working and I swoop into turns two and three (turn one was not really a corner, just a crook in the road at start-finish. Flat out.

Then going up the hill into six I pass a slew and within two laps I have the lead. Man that was fun!

Long story short, I finally won my first race of the season. Happiness is way too weak a word to describe the feeling standing in victory circle with a gorgeous blonde, my sweet equally gorgeous wife, a bottle of champagne, and a huge trophy and a million or two fans and sponsor reps.

The TRACO engine had performed flawlessly; gauges were normal all the way and power never diminished. I sent a telegram to Jim Travers Monday morning, which was the day after the US holiday Mother's day; the telegram read in part "Strong Mother's Day!"

Of course I had no idea that following all that celebration would come utter disaster.

On the way across country heading to the next race, an idiot crew member badly misjudged his stamina, and fell asleep at the wheel in Utah. The enclosed trailer ended up on its side, the camper top on the truck spilled all its guts and thousands of dollars' worth of spares were embedded in the dirt and dust beside the road.

Nickey Chevrolet, our primary sponsor, immediately sprung into action. The head of the competition division at Nickey, Al

Seelig, sprung for a new truck in Utah and the crew picked up the pieces and hit the road again.

Here's where it gets really freaking weird.

I am in Chicago, waiting for the rig to show up, when I get a phone call. The same damn crew member, who I have a very hard time forgiving, had done the same thing in Nebraska, falling asleep again and crashing! And this time weakening some of the suspension on the car as it flailed about in the trailer. More about that later.....

I was more than devastated; it was like descending into hell after visiting heaven. I went from hero to zero and then way down from there in one horrible couple of days.

Al was devastated too of course. But he got another new truck in Nebraska as well. We limped back to Chicago and cleaned up as best we could but of course our season was ruined. But on we went....

After cleaning up the mess as best we could we headed up to Ste Jovite for a non-championship pro event for Group Seven/USRRC cars. On arrival we discovered that the lower right rear suspension "wishbone".... a critical piece.... had bloody well broken on the trailer!

Imagine if that sucker had busted say in turn one at Ste Jovite at a hundred plus! I shudder still at that possibility!

In any event I sought out Bruce McLaren as I believed that his car used the same part. I asked him if he could loan us a spare. He replied, "bit late in the game for that isn't it!?" I thought that was uncharacteristic for Bruce. So much for customer service! So we had to settle for getting the thing welded together again in town. But the car never felt right the whole weekend.

I qualified mid pack: Sam Posey was directly in front of us on the grid, and Sam strolled back to me and said he would let me by no problem. But being able to actually GET by, well that was quite another matter. The car was crap all weekend. Out of alignment, bump steering, loose as a buckboard on glare ice! I don't remember if or where we finished.

We took out for Bridgehampton's USRRC anyway, and that was another disaster. We could not get the car to handle at all and it scared the shit out of me especially in turn one, a sweeping very fast downhill right hander. Desperate for some fix we borrowed Mark Donohue's Dunlop alignment tools. No help at all. Finally we gave up and headed back to the coast with a screwed up car and a whole lot of disappointment.

Fast & Faster!

Frankly, up until the Road America 500 finale the remainder of the USRRC season is a blur! Then we lost the race at Elkhart by four one thousandth of a second after leading the entire race until the last 1/16th of a mile.

But THAT is another tale.

After a semi-disastrous total season to date with the #97 car we finally made it to Elkhart Lake for the final USRRC race, a 500 miler. While prepping the car in the Nickey Chevrolet shops in Chicago, we got word that the great Ken Miles, the lead driver for Shelby America, the Cobra manufacturer, had gotten killed testing a Ford race carat Riverside, California. This was devastating news!

I knew Ken and felt close to him as he had been my team leader when I drove the #95 Cobra at Bridgehampton, in the World Championship race. I fondly recall Ken knocking on my door on race morning with a cheery "Wakey-Wakey!"

And it would begin to eat away at my determination as yet another racer was killed. I began to believe way back in a corner of the mind that just maybe, I could indeed get bumped off that way too.

But I still manage to mostly suppress those feelings, at least for now....

Carl Haas, the McLaren importer, had with great generosity loaned me another McLaren M1B to use, which was fortunate since my original car was really a mess. We had gotten the #97 working reasonably well, but never close to like it was out of the gate at Riverside and Laguna.

Carl told me that if I won the race, he would have his tailor make me a suit. Carl's tailor was awesome, so I really wanted that outfit. Deep side vents and all. I was already wearing the sucker in my mind!

We had prepared the car well, with help from two good drivers, John Morton and Earl Jones, and new chief mechanic Larry Burton, at Nickey's shops in Chicago. I wanted a co-driver for the 500, and as luck would have it I had two great ones to choose from.

I picked Earl Jones because I had seen him drive a Genie Can-Am car and he seemed to be both quick AND easy on the equipment. Since we were already thousands in the red that was very damn important!

The Carl Haas #98 McLaren was a piece of cake to prepare and we went up to Elkhart feeling very good about the car for a change, and in fact easily won the pole with a new lap record. As the race started I jumped out to a good lead over a strong field. And really being easy on the ride. My confidence soared as we covered a hundred, then a hundred fifty miles. Easy peasy!

I gave the car to Earl around the hundred fifty mile mark for a short middle stint. Refueling went without a hitch and Earl did a great job before giving me the car back with about 200 miles to go.

Then later the excrement hit the rotating device and stunk everything up! More on that shortly....

Now it's only a hundred or so miles to the end of the five hundred. And all is going very well indeed. Thanks, in large measure, to the great talents and hard work of our new Crew Chief Larry Burton.

Larry joined us in California after the original bloke and I rather vehemently agreed we should disagree. He had lost any passion he might have had and went several days without coming to work on the #97 car at all, complaining about sunburn. He had time for the sun and sand at Newport Beach but not for the racing team. And I had every penny I owned in this car.

Really disheartening all around.

I don't recall now exactly how Larry, a great guy who had the fire to win despite being wheelchair bound (!) joined us. We then went to Kent for the USRRC and did a DNF, then next to Mid-Ohio for another USRRC event; I don't remember how that went so it likely wasn't real awesome!

Anyway, Larry towed to Elkhart from the Nickey shops and set out to get the #98 Haas car set up to last 500 miles. He did exactly that but the engine was not under his aegis. That was Traco, the California engine builder who had a rep for power and reliability.

But as I told an interviewer on television these cars and engines were not really designed for 500 mile races.

To get back to the race, around 400 in, I began to notice slight elevations in the water and mostly, the oil temperature. This I thought was surely a small anomaly and the very reliable Traco 333 Strong Mother would surely go another measly 100 damn miles ya would think huh?

The motor racing gods must have been laughing their fool heads off!

Pretty soon the temperature elevations were no longer slight but large size and climbing. Then the oil pressure started dropping and the engine went onto seven cylinders. Shit no! This can NOT be happening, I thought.

So very soon, maybe at mile 450, it was into the pits to have a few quarts of oil added. Larry's pick up crew member, a good man named Mike Sheridan who I knew from my Maryland home track, braved the brutal heat to add oil.

We still had a huge lead so off we went to the war running on seven. But we were losing time every lap to USRRC points leader Chuck Parsons who was in a solid second. Good friend. Good driver. Good engine man. Built one for the 500 mile race, he did. But obviously my enemy on the racetrack today!

The bloody thing ran worse and worser and another stop for oil was needed (maybe two, if memory serves.... not sure). In any case Parsons was gaining by big chunks and there was not one goddam thing I could do about it!

Frustrated. Pissed to the moon. Enraged. All the words are way too weak to capture the enormity of emotions I was feeling. But I was still leading!

Until the very last lap.

Coming up to the finish the engine just went even flatter and Chuck roared to a finish.... get this.... Four One Thousandths of a second ahead.... to freaking beat us by inches.

I thought my head would explode.

Second place, my friends, is First Loser. Full Stop.

Larry, Mike and Earl were equally devastated. And my wife Evey was totally at a loss for words too. This was a moment over which we would NEVER get. As I write this I am still pissed! Well, not really....

No one over-revved the engine. There was no abuse. We ran to finish, just fast enough. Some F1 builder or driver once said the idea was to have everything fall apart and win by one second at the checker. Might have been Colin Chapman of Lotus. But to paraphrase some currently famous person, "what difference, at this point, does it make!?"

So that's racing. The most elevating and devastating sport the human animal has ever known.

I salute Larry, Earl, Mike and Evey for their commitment, passion and hard work. The fond memories of them make the loss almost bearable. To this day I remember that race as both my toughest and, ironically, my finest.

That, my friends is Racin'! As I have had to intone many, many times.

After Elkhart would come the Can-Am, the Canadian American Challenge Cup series for Group Seven cars like ours. These races would attract stars from all types of racing; Indy, Formula One, the USRRC and more. "All the cars and all the stars" our friend Tyler Alexander of McLaren would say jokingly form time to time. All the best guys like the 1965 pro races were contested by.

We had started the program in the spring with the Can-Am in mind but by the time of the first event at Ste. Jovite we were way far less than competitive against the world class field of top notch cars and hot shoes. Having fired our original mechanics because of aforementioned certain lack of enthusiasm / competence didn't help either. There were zero results, a string of Did Not Finish happenings that ate up the budget and generally left us discouraged, especially after the Elkhart 500 loss.

In any case went on to Bridgehampton, Mosport, Laguna Seca, Riverside, and Las Vegas, where we at best ran mid pack before again failing to finish. I would be happy to share the details of these events, but I honestly don't remember them at all.

After such a promising beginning despite failures in the first two USRRC races we were devastated. And broke, until Brett

Lunger, a member of the DuPont family, crashed his Lola in practice and so came to me and bought the original #97 car (I was running Carl Haas' #98 car) from me for a good amount of money.

We returned Carl's car to him and went back to Maryland licking our wounds. Terrible year! Bu that money from Brett for the #97 paid our bills for the next few months and allowed us to make a long desired move to Southern California, at the time the epicenter of racing. Partly due to the aerospace industry which we certainly drew on heavily. We rented a nice apartment in Orange near the upscale shopping center, Fashion Park. Nice area, nice flat. Our new SoCal home.

Chapter 10: 1967

We got our move done and settled in to Southern California in the spring of 1967, with no ride and no job. I had asked Bob McKee of Palatine Illinois, a well-known race car builder, to get a McKee Mk.7 ready for me but sponsorship fell through and Bob ended up selling the car to club racer Ralph Salyer of Hammond, Indiana. Ralph and his partner Gene Crowe had formed "Cro-Sal Racing" and were winners in their own right. This would prove beneficial to me later that year….

Meanwhile I had a privateer McKee owner named Tod Oseid contact me about running his car in a few select races, which I did but with no results of any note save for one 2nd place at Wilmot in Illinois.. We did take the car to Kent near Seattle for a USRRC but ended up with yet another DNF with a punctured gas tank. Believe it or not I had somehow left a screwdriver loose in the cockpit. It went unnoticed until it lodged itself betwixt race track and tank. Instant hole. Gas running out. Stupid was I. DNF obviously.

Meanwhile, to make a little money I began selling racing equipment, first out of my apartment, then out of a small shop in industrial Santa Ana. We did a few braided steel hose jobs, notably Teflon/Stainless Dash Three brake hoses for Dan Gurney's All American Racers. Evey went to work as a bank teller. We adopted a dog that two kids were trying to hang, outside the Bank where Evey worked. She ran out and rescued him, cute little guy that looked like a miniature Corgi. We named him Zeus. Father of Apollo, king of the gods!

Memories are dim here regarding exactly where and when we raced the Tod Oseid McKee and exactly when Ralph Salyer called and invited me to drive the Cro-Sal McKee Oldsmobile (I think it was early August) but no call was ever more welcome given my frustrations with the Oseid car. Poor Tod was a great guy but there was no budget for such things as TRACO engines!

A note here: I don't know how Evey stood it; I was super depressed except when I was in a race car and there were pretty much no race cars through July 1967, except for the uncombative Oseid McKee….

Motor Racing: the most exhilarating and heartbreaking endeavor one can imagine.

But Ralph called, and I had a ride at least for Mid-Ohio's August 1965 USRRC race and the intimation was there would be a lot more. I hopped up the car by phone with Gene Crowe; getting all the specs for springs, anti-roll bars and suspension I then obtained very stiff springs and big huge anti-roll bars for the car and brought them on the airplane with me to Hammond Indiana, where Ralph had his shop and plumbing business. And I came on board to the team with my Bump Steer Alignment equipment.

Yes, I was applying all I learned from Trevor Harris even then! And it was easy to get all that built in Southern California. Plus Ralph and Gene were amazingly open to what I wanted to do. Neat!

Gene and Ralph had a connection at Oldsmobile, an engineer named Dale Smith, lovely guy, smart as a whip, who got the works to cast up some big alloy Olds engine blocks and heads for them. 442 if I remember rightly.

These engines were, well, almost competitive with the TRACO small block mills of the time, but not quite. Noble effort though by all involved! But the big block super Chevys from TRACO were to be impossible to run with, in the Can-Am to come....

Anyway, we worked three days straight and were very late getting to Ohio, arriving Saturday afternoon well after practice was finished and right at the start of qualifying.

I had no problem going fast on Mid Ohio's great road course, and in qualifying we outran all but Mark Donohue in his impeccable Penske Lola T70. A front row start for my first real race of the year. I was really alive and happy for a change!

That qualifier shocked a few people especially since we had driven all night to get there and I had had no sleep for 30 hours or more!

As the race started I diced a bit with Chuck Parsons in Carl Haas' McLaren, and with Donohue, but Mark soon pulled away and left me a mile behind him.... but a mile ahead of everyone else. The car worked really well on the twists and turns of Mid-Ohio and I was in a state of pure peace as I thrust the thing around, drifting, powering through corners, trail barking into the turns and standing on it out onto the ensuing straights.

This, I knew, I was born to do.

The race went on with no incidents as I lapped slower cars and stood fast in second behind Mark, when just two corners before the checkered flag the damn thing sputtered and stopped, out of gas! How in hell?

Well, talk about being devastated, it was like Elkhart '66 all over again. The original McKee tank was just that bit too small for a thirsty Gene Crowe Olds motor. Wow.

After the walk back to the pits I was inundated with well-wishers, and one press guy who seemed open, whom I told that Donohue could really drive! He told Mark later, who said, "Charlie said that!?" Yes, I was a bit more respectful at this stage; slightly less arrogant or so I hoped.

Next up would be Bridgehampton, a fast sandy course out at the tip of long Island, New York. I gotten to almost like the Bridge, even the somewhat intimidating turn one, a sweeper to the right and downhill, off camber, no guard rails, just sandy shoulders one did NOT want to go off in!

That turn was like a roller coaster downhill; the car tried to run off to the left because of the reverse camber – the road sloped the wrong way. The McKee was loose in that turn going 120 MPH probably. That kept me awake I must say.

We had a fair lap time going, at 11th quick which considering the competition and our lack of horses was not all that bad, when the only engine we had swallowed a part of itself to its great detriment. In the parlance, it dropped a damn valve. We were a small team with no spare engine so that was that for the weekend.

But along the way I had met a nice guy in Los Angeles, named Hugh Powell who was racing a Lola T70. He had The

Smothers Brothers Comedy Hour logo and script on his car. We became friends and Hugh introduced me to Dickie Smothers, and that developed into a solid friendship, then a relationship as a "sponsor".... the name and fame was figured to gain money sponsors.

We didn't ask the Smothers for money; that we would get from, for example, Goodyear who appreciated that relationship. We got to go to CBS and see the live taping of The Comedy Hour a couple of times and saw the cast backstage; this was a kick and three quarters!

Bridgehampton was the first race where we had The Smothers Brothers livery so it was a damn shame we could not run due to the busted motor. Yes I know…. That's Racing!

Next up was the great Mosport track up near Toronto. But that was not what could be called an auspicious event!

(Note: Parts of this chapter appeared in my book "Life After Death" in 2006 but the date of the happening was wrong. The Mosport events happened in 1967, not 1968 as mistakenly stated in "Life After Death." Apologies!)

It was qualifying for the September 1967 Can-Am, the Canadian American Challenge Cup. This round was at Mosport Park, near Toronto. One of my all-time favorite racetracks.

Fast & Faster!

Uphill and down, fast sweeping off camber bends. A racer's Paradise.

We're being timed, for the best one lap of balls to the wall racing against the clock trying to set a single hot lap that the others guys can't match. The race car is working better than it ever has and I am stoked. This was the happiest moment of my life. Superstar Peter Revson was there that day driving a factory McLaren, and I found myself dicing with him for maybe 6th on the grid. Bruce McLaren himself was there. And a lot of other great drivers.

Legendary Formula One, Indy 500 Stars are here racing today! I am an upstart among legends - a hopefully rising star among superstars.

We knew we had no chance for the pole. I was a good racer, but if I were to make a truthful assessment, I was not all that great against Formula One stars like Bruce McLaren, F1 Champ John Surtees, Bob Bondurant, Graham Hill, also an F1 Champ, and great Sports Car Aces like Jim Hall, Mark Donohue, Lothar Motschenbacher, and all that lot.

Not only that, but our small team with its lone race car, and single motor, committed though we were, and fast and nimble though our car was, certainly was NO match for the highly sponsored factory McLarens, Lolas and Chaparrals. We were realistic about that. So I was not altogether displeased around sixth at this stage and hoping simply to stay there, or maybe get up to fifth.

I was standing on it. Turning into a downhill left-hander at about 120 MPH. The car was stable as I bent the thing into the turn, all four wheels loose in a controlled drift. As the apex comes up in this corner, the hilltop crests and starts to sharply slope down toward the hairpin turn at the bottom, "Moss' Corner." It's a little bit off camber, and the car gets very, very light at this point.

Drifting, flat out, I was in heaven. There were no limits. I was "Home" (so I thought, because I "knew" this "experience of Oneness" was "home")....

I was flying, supremely free.

Man, was I ever Awake and Alive.

There was no mind, no thought, just … an "experience (only an experience) of BEING. Being.... Fully Awake and Fully Alive.

It was Bliss. Total Joy. Total Freedom. Flying all alone at the speed of light. There was nobody in the car. It was all oneness and Simple Being.... free and unbounded. I was no longer

Fast & Faster!

Charlie. I was EVERYTHING. The Car. The Road. The Sunny Cloudless Sky.

Then in one Instant outside of Time it was all over.

Suddenly.... Bang!

There is a loud cracking sound. Then all at once there is nothing.

Not Blackness. Not even that!

I and world are gone.

Everything - is gone.

Deep sleep death.

Much later I am told that a hub carrier, an alloy casting that holds the wheel to the suspension, had broken, and the right rear wheel had immediately come off, which sent the car out of control and careening toward God Only Knew What.

It ended up against a dirt bank, backwards, in Moss' corner

Later I heard that everyone who saw the crash was aghast, as they saw a 'lifeless' form slumped in the cockpit and they "knew" that Charlie is Dead! There was much shaking of heads, and "Wow, how terrible," uttered, as the medics gathered up the lifeless organism and bundled it sadly into the meat wagon.

For about an hour, as time measured the instant, the Charlie entity was totally gone. Then Charlie came back, but who Charlie was for himself and others as a racer had died forever, when the car hit an earth bank at Moss' Corner backwards, still going probably 100 MPH. Since I hit backwards and not front first, I am still here! The engine and gearbox, in the back of course, took the brunt. My head smacked the roll bar and that was a good-night moment.

As a friend, Frank Gardner, once said, "That nasty business of going from 100 MPH to ZERO is just a bit hard on the old nervous system."

Tell me about it. This body has had backaches and headaches for over 48 years.

At the time: I awake to see the kind and concerned face of my Crew Chief, Gene Crowe, gazing at me. As he sees my eyes open he grins in relief.

The first thing I say is, "How bad is the car? Can we run tomorrow?"

Gene and everyone else laughed a little nervously at that. The car would take a month or so to rebuild; it was a close to a total loss as a car can get without actually being a total.

Then I try to get up.

My head swims, my legs feel like water. I learn later I had gotten quite a serious concussion. When the car hit, my head was thrown back hard against the roll bar. The helmet evidently saved my physical life.... but that was questionable, as it turned out.... from my perspective now, I cannot know WHAT saved the life of that body!

But nothing could have saved my Racing Life. This was the first blow wherein I started to lose confidence in both myself and the cars. I would go on through 1968 but I was NOT the same guy after this crash. I have always admired guys that seemed unaffected by accidents like this who went on the win again and again. Mario Andretti comes to mind here. And John Surtees.

That helmet was sent off for testing as required in all serious crashes, and the report came back, "The guy in that busted crash helmet could not possibly have lived through that crash."

Indeed. Upright and half dead

To paraphrase that famous Steve McQueen quote, "Life was in the Race Car. Everything else was just waiting."

The repairs took quite a while as the car was damn near a total as I noted, so our next event would be Laguna Seca. We ran a good lap there, around 1:04, good enough for 8th on a grid full of stars. But the car felt a little off; at one point in practice the steering locked up, that was scary. It was fixed easily though and we motored on….

We didn't finish at Laguna though I don't recall why; one record said we had an accident but I don't recall that at all. Hmmmm.

After Laguna came Riverside for the Lost Angeles Times Grand Prix, and this was another favorite track. For the Can-Am we would run the long course at Riverside which gave us about a full mile back straight. I was powering through turn eight and down that straight at about 160 when a huge dust cloud enveloped me and completely obscured the track from view. I didn't back off though, rather dumbly I kept my foot down and whooshed through the thing wherein fortunately there was nothing to run into! Wow.

Given we were competing against world class drivers in cars that in some cases had like 100 more horsepower (big block TRACO Chevrolet engines for example) I was happy to come in 7th. Our little team was doing okay! Even with the fading confidence I was experiencing. And Dickie Smothers seemed to be having a good time. (Later he would start driving himself and he turned out to be quite quick!)

Fast & Faster!

Speaking of that, Dickie would call and invite us to his house for dinner, and to shoot some pool – he had a gorgeous house and a pro class pool table. Another time he invited us to join him at a five star restaurant in Orange called Villa Fontana where there was to be a start studded fashion show. Perks of having a TV star friend indeed.

He was never anything but this really nice, sharp guy and we were privileged to call Dickie and Linda friends.

Another time he invited us to a posh private club called The Factory, which was situated on a side street in Los Angeles; no signs, no paparazzi, nothing but what looked like an empty warehouse. We rode up to the club itself in a freight elevator!

The stunning sight of Henry Fonda playing pool and so many other mega-stars that I lost count brought me to a full stop. What a life I was having; Evey and I had never been exposed to such insider stardom indeed. We were so stoked!

As to the season of Can-Am, by far our best result came at Las Vegas. We had a good car for the course and qualified well toward the front. After a delightful dinner out with Dickie and his then wife Linda, Evey and I felt like we had sort of "arrived".

As the race started on Sunday I sort of watched as the rev counter rose to 7000, then a gear shift up, then back up to 7000, passing cars easily. The engine sounded like a p51 Mustang, music to me.

Sliding slightly through the sandy corners – won't do to go off here, or here – and clipping corners just past the geometrical apex, turning in and light braking and accelerating out all in one smooth motion – as I watch my hands steer, shift up and down, all in a cloud of natural knowing what's next, being three corners ahead of the present moments at the same time as working the current turn, time standing outside itself, presence wider and wider. All on a kind of peaceful blissful auto-happening.

Little by little we climbed up the charts and finally found ourselves in Fourth, and considering the international field of stars we thought this was not a bad result at all. The team was happy. I was exhausted, used up completely, and happy as a groom on his wedding night. Oh yeah, Evey was there too so after the race we fulfilled that wedding night idea which started as a metaphor and ended up as a passionate happening!

A very fulfilling final to the weekend, and we ended in a tie with Parnelli Jones and Peter Revson for 9th in the Can-Am Championship. Not bad for a little team from Indiana eh?

Especially after nearly demolishing the car (and the driver!) at Mosport.

Later in December, Ralph, Gene and I went up to Lansing, Michigan to meet our pal Dale Smith, to look at the engine program for 1968. But that turned into like a three day visit as we got thoroughly snowed in by a blizzard of epic proportions.

Later that winter Gene and I sat in a restaurant and sketched out a wedge shaped body design for the 1968 season—on cocktail napkins! We later passed them on to Bob McKee with a simple request: Build this please.

He did.

Chapter 11: 1968

In February 1968, Don Nichols (later to be of Shadow Can Am and F1 fame) called me from Tokyo, to let me know that he was arranging for me to come to Japan test and tweak the Nissan R 381 race car. Don had been a customer of my small company Hayes Racing Equipment: we sold Hewland gearboxes and other racing supplies and Don was selling my stuff in Japan and doing quite a good business there, as he was also the Firestone racing tire distributor.

This was quite an opportunity for me, first off because I had never been to Japan and I looked forward to that, but also because Nissan was very serious about winning the Japan Grand prix and beating Toyota, coming up later that year.

Don, who lived in Japan at that time, was very good friends with the chief engineer for the project, one S. Sakurai. He had brought Sakurai to my shop in California earlier that year, with the drawings of the R 381 suspension. I pointed out to Sakurai that his rear suspension as designed would produce a lot of camber change, seriously affecting the stickability of the rear tires!

I showed him a simple change, merely relocating the upper inboard pickup point about 2 inches higher, and plotted the now nonexistent camber change on bump and rebound. There were grins all around! I had learned this from my friend Trevor Harris, who had applied the fix to my 1965 McLaren, with incredibly good results.

The problem was, I had a baby due on the date of the test, March 17th, 1968. What to do? While negotiations were going on, my wife talked to her gynecologist, who informed her it would be perfectly safe to induce labor, and have the baby, on March 10th. So this meant I could be there, and even have a few days with her and the baby before departing for Japan. Solution found!

Don got back to me and said that he was negotiating for a personal services fee which I found perfectly satisfactory, as well as first-class fare from LA to Japan. He said he did not expect that they would do first-class, it was a negotiating point. I was very pleasantly surprised when Nissan came back with the offer for the requested fee plus first class air travel!

So shortly after the baby was born, I found myself on a first-class Pan Am jet that flew to Tokyo by way of Anchorage, Alaska. I got off the plane in Anchorage and walked around in the terminal, fascinated by the gigantic stuffed polar bear guarding the terminal.

Fast & Faster!

Getting back on the plane, I relaxed in great comfort and for the next several hours was extremely well taken care of by the flight crew. What a trip!

Arriving in Tokyo, as I got off of the plane, which had steps, not an airway; I was greeted by a sign with my name on it, and a chauffeur who would take me into town to meet the Nissan executives. There were photographers and all also. I felt like a rock star.

Arriving at the Tokyo Ginzu hotel, in the vibrant Ginza district, I was greeted by senior executives from Nissan, who escorted me to my sumptuous hotel room. As they had me ensconced comfortably, they then asked me, is there anything else you need? I replied no. This all looks fine.

One of the executives looked at me quizzically, and said "not need woman?" I said, politely but emphatically, "no thanks!" I had a beautiful wife and a new baby at home. I was not gonna mess with that.

I awakened in the land of the rising Sun with mixed feelings! My father had lost his life in World War II when his ship, the Indianapolis, was hit by a Japanese torpedo. I had to put these feelings aside and concentrate on the job at hand, which was to be with the Nissan executives, some of whom had participated in World War II, and focus on the testing and sorting out of the R381 racecar.

My main concern would be proving out that the suspension changes, along with the recommendation for very big anti-roll bars front and rear, and some possible spring adjustments, had been carried out. I soon found out that they had and in fact been impeccably done.

The same executives met me in the morning and took me to the Nissan headquarters, where I was escorted to the top floor boardroom, and treated to a genuine tea ceremony. No business was discussed for a good hour. This was the civilization of the Japanese culture, which I could deeply appreciate, and it helped me forget about my dad.

We then departed for the racing team headquarters, which was in a very large building which contained not only the cars and the engineers but a gigantic supercomputer. Mr. Sakurai and team had been using the computer to plot the possible braking points and corner speeds at Fuji Speedway, for the R381. Among other things. This was a very sophisticated operation! Yet Mr. Sakurai was quite humble and open to my suggestions, as he had been in California.

Fast & Faster!

As things unfolded, it seemed we would not be visiting the racetrack for yet another day or so. This was fine with me, because although I was anxious to get to the racetrack, and drive the R381, I still had a bit of jet lag going on. I should note here that some of the events I am about to share, I do not know the exact chronology of; memory fails. So I am going to use a little writer's discretion and place them as best I can. Starting with, a very pleasant visit to a wonderful place called Atami Spa! The baths at this place were coeducational, the ladies on one side and the men on the other.

As I stripped off my clothes to get into the men's side, the executives were giggling as they knew I was a bit shy to expose myself. However, the steam was so thick from the hot water that we could not see the other side. But there certainly were a lot of giggles from the female side, because the word had evidently gotten out that there was some sort of gringo semi-celebrity was in attendance that day!

I had been informed that Japanese Playboy had taken a keen interest! My first exposure to paparazzi! Pictures taken with a million millimeter telephoto lens at the speedway would appear on the magazine cover!

That Atami place was very invigorating and helped to cure some of the jet lag, leaving me with the realization that these

Fast & Faster!

Japanese executives were really smart. They knew bloody well I would have jet lag! And they set up a schedule so that it would not be a factor in my help making their race cars fast enough to ultimately beat Toyota, which they did a couple of years later..

Next on the agenda was a wonderful dinner with Don Nichols, his wife, and Mr. Sakurai. I remember experiencing Kobe beef for the first time. So succulent and tender. Unforgettable. It was a very pleasant time, and all were amused at my feeble attempts to speak Japanese. The resentment regarding my father was pretty well gone. But it might just be revisited later!

The next day, we still did not go to the Speedway. Frankly, I have forgotten how we spent the day. But I remember it as being pleasant. The jet lag had just about disappeared and I felt very fit and healthy.

I do recall the executives taking me to lunch at a place in Ginza that served live crayfish. Uh Oh!! Also, I bumped my 6ft 3in head going in, of course. Ha!

When my plate arrived with the living critters on it crawling around, the executives all gave me great attention, wondering if I was going to eat the damn things. One of them giggled and said not yet asleep. Asleep came up "asreep!" Honestly, I do not remember eating one but I think I did, because I remember some looks of admiration from the Japanese executives. Such is life in the big city of Tokyo!

Finally, we would be going to the circuit. The following day. I was eagerly anticipating a lot of fun and some good work to be done. I was very much looking forward to meeting the Japanese drivers, and the pit crew for the two R381's, which would appear at the tests.

But first was a very strange dinner that night in a five star restaurant with the Nissan Elite:

It was finally just a few hours before we would get up the mountain to run the R381s at Fuji Speedway! I was more than ready; it was like Christmas Eve for me. But first, there was to be a wonderful dinner with about a dozen Nissan executives; it seemed like the entire board was there. And at a five-star restaurant to boot. Sakurai-San was not there, clearly off getting ready for the test session to follow early the next day.

About halfway through a very pleasant meal, wherein the conversations were mainly about winning the Japan Grand Prix, the conversation turned to World War II and these men's participation in it, flying Mitsubishi aircraft. I really had to hold my tongue. Because, as mentioned before, my father was on the Indianapolis, which was sunk two weeks before the end of the war by the last Japanese submarine in the Pacific Ocean!

Somehow though, I realized that if I had been a Japanese sitting at a table full of American flyers the conversation would have been very likely the same. These guys just loved flying fast moving aircraft. In that way, they were kind of a family to me, and I could not find them to be wrong. They were just guys like me, albeit a lot older!

So the dinner finished up with a wonderful dessert and lots of handshakes and bows all around. They returned me to my sumptuous hotel room, where I went to sleep anticipating driving, at last, the next day.

Early the next morning, like oh dark 30, a car and driver was waiting to drive me up to Fuji Speedway. He would take one small side trip, in order to show me some of the little volcano eruptions that occurred on the side of Mount Fuji in numerous quantity. Fascinating.

Arriving at the Speedway, I was introduced to the crew, by Sakurai himself, as well as the drivers testing that day with me, Moto Kitano and (I do not remember his first name) Takahashi.... Takahashi was very friendly and we hit it off straight away. I enjoyed our somewhat stilted conversations,

Fast & Faster!

with his broken English and my broken Japanese! It did not matter, we were instant brothers. Moto Kitano was another matter. He was quite reserved, and clearly was concentrating on the job at hand, to the exclusion of irrelevant conversations.

But both of these men were racers. Make no mistake.

It was a typical Japanese March day at Fuji, cloudy and threatening rain. Almost drizzly, the humidity was palpable. I was a bit concerned because there were no full rain tires brought to the test, we would run solely on the Don Nichols supplied Firestone dry and intermediate weather tires. So be it.

The cars were ready, and the two Japanese drivers went out to shake them down, make sure all the bits and pieces were solidly fastened down. Then it was my turn. The team had done their best to adjust the cockpit for my 6'3" frame, but I've got to tell you it was a very, very tight squeeze! That said, as soon as I fired up and engaged first gear and took off, I forgot about all that.

As I accelerated down toward turn one and shifting without the clutch as I had prepared the glass bead-blasted and modified dog ring Hewland gearboxes to be able to do, I was back in my element at last.

By the time I bent the car around turn one, luxuriating in the good handling, I knew this race car would work. This was going to be a winner! Being new to Fuji Speedway, I took a few laps to acclimate myself and make sure my assessment was valid, and sure enough, the R381 was perfectly set up. And I was amazed how close the computer simulations were to the actual braking points and shifting points. The gear ratios were perfect. This was a car done up by a VERY good team!

I do not know what top speed was but I would guess around the 170-180 Mark. Man, this car was stable. Even though the wing that would be affixed for the Grand prix had yet to be installed.

An interesting note, these were coupes. Sakurai-San would remove the tops for the Japan Grand Prix and have an open cockpit racecar, similar to the competing Toyota 7, with a wing added. But the chassis, engine and gearbox, in other words the whole car except for the bodywork, would remain the same.

After a few laps, I turned the car back over to the team drivers, then relaxed over a cup of coffee, chatting with Mr. Sakurai. I was having a great time. Could have done this for a month.

The day went along that way, quite laid-back considering what was at stake for Nissan, yet there was an underlying urgent commitment to have these cars work 100%. So the testing continued into the afternoon. I turned a few more laps but as far as I was concerned, nothing needed to be tweaked. We retired for the evening and made our way back to Tokyo for a pleasant dinner with Don Nichols and his wife at Don's lovely apartment in central Tokyo.

Early the next morning we would go at it again. But it was a drizzly day all the way up the mountain and the track was damp approaching wet, and again we had no rain tires. But we soldiered on, of course. After the team drivers had run a few laps, I took over one of the cars and found it to be a bit dicey in the wet, which was to be expected.

Then after a few fun laps, on the back side of the circuit, in a beautiful downhill sweeping turn, I discovered a river running across the racetrack at the bottom of the hill. Oops. I spun 360°, and had some sweat spots under the armpits of my Goodyear driving suit! I motored back up the hill to the pits, got out of the car, and suggested to Sakurai that since we had no full rain tires it would probably be best to curtail the test at this point.

I reminded him as far as I was concerned the cars were fine and would be highly competitive anywhere.

But Moto Kitano was not having any of it!

He immediately jumped in the car and took off like a scalded cat, running up through the gears and going nearly flat through turn one. He did a couple of laps like that but on somewhere around the third or fourth lap, in the long right turn heading into the pits he spun wildly and crashed into the barrier under the timing stand. And the damn car caught fire!

I was not about to say I told you so, but I had to say, "Too bad to lose a car." Sakurai simply said, with a shrug of the shoulders, "We'll build another one." It was clearly no big deal to them! Welcome to the era of huge budgets!

At that point we were done for the day and despite the loss of a car everyone was very, very pleased. I relaxed and napped on the drive back to the hotel, looking forward to a good rest. I would be departing next day on a Pan Am jet to Los Angeles, I was looking forward to getting home to the family.

All in all I was deeply amazed and had great respect for the Team and Drivers as well as the Crew and Designers. Especially Mr. Sakurai. And Don Nichols, for having arranged this great week for me. And as it turned out, the aggressive and committed Kitano went on to ultimately win the Japan Grand Prix. That was after all the point. Well done! The car was right, he was right, the team was right, and it was a privilege for me to have been a small part of all of that.

Fast & Faster!

After the race, I received a signed photograph of the R382, the evolution of the R381, winning the 1970 Japan GP from Mr. Sakurai, expressing their thanks for my input, which is buried somewhere in the archives and clippings of my career that my son has stored.

In any case I was very happy to get home to my new family, and relate some of the stories to my wife, who, as I was, was quite amazed at the unfolding of all of that.

Then there was this cute little boy….

Then in late March or early April I was running my small racing equipment business when I got a call from Bob Bondurant, the great driver who, after a bad crash, had started a driving school. He was training movie and TV personalities to drive in crazy film scenes as well as training racing drivers in his unique methods to go fast and faster. Great coach, this man.

Anyway Bob asked me if I could bring the new McKee Mark 10 "Wedge" to Elkhart Lake for a filming. Universal Studios was shooting a new movie called "Winning" starring Paul Newman, Joanne Woodward and Robert (RJ) Wagner. I told Bob that it was fine with me but I needed to ask Ralph and Gene if this was something they wanted to do. Ralph and Gene immediately said, you bet! Let's do it.

Fast & Faster!

So we went up to Elkhart Lake with our new McKee Mk. 10 "Wedge" anticipating a fun and productive week. We needed to test the thing anyway and this was a way to get paid for doing it. How cool was that!

The wedge was an immediate attraction, drawing the movie people to it, especially Paul Newman. Paul was so NOT a movie star in attitude: Just a real, authentic, regular guy, albeit very sharp indeed. We hit it off right away and I am happy to assert that we became friends straight away. Great guy. Wagner was also neat, and not stuck up at all. I did not meet Joanne Woodward, unfortunately; she was in none of the scenes for the film at the race track, which was where all our action was.

The Elkhart segment was the opening sequence for "Winning" which would go on to Indy later. Essentially, "Winning" was a love story about racers. I thought that was mega cool!

Frankly, I was blown away by the scene. Hanging out with Newman, Wagner and the movie people was a season in heaven. Ralph and Gene and I had never had it so good as when Dickie Smothers came on board, and this was a magnificent extension of that great fun.

Fast & Faster!

Gene had the car impeccably prepared, and Newman was rather taken with it. As the week developed Paul expressed the desire that the McKee be the car he drove in the movie. We all readily agreed. Paul had been coached by some good drivers so we had no concerns there, plus this was a very sane guy and we knew he'd keep it on the highways of Elkhart. At least, that's what we guessed. After all, this was our Can-Am car for 1968; we couldn't afford to lose it or have a repeat of Mosport 1967!

We had some open practice that I was able to test the car in and I found it to be trouble free. This was the first outing for the Mk. 10 so we needed to check all the usual systems, gearbox, steering, bump steer and so on. We had use of the garage building at the track so we could get it all done right there; very convenient.

The weather was beautiful, very spring like and mostly sunny. (To tell the truth memory fails here regarding dates. I think this must have been April though I suppose it could have been late April or early May. But that doesn't matter now.)

Four miles through rolling country, through trees and delicious corners, a perfect place to play. Front pit straight into two fast rights onto long back straight leading to a hard left, maybe 60 MPH in a Can-Am car. Up a lazy hill to a left and right that dumped one onto a turn called the Carrousel, a long decreasing radius right that exited onto a fast slightly bent straightaway through a forest of green; down to a quick right and up a hill into a left, then a right hander onto the pit straight. We could get to 170 in places including the pit straight! One of the best road courses in the world. (That is what a 48 year old memory gives me as a lap around the place; I might have a section or two a little off. So what, he said, glowering about faulty memory in the dark and then grinning.)

Bondurant had collected about 12 Can-Am cars for this segment of "Winning" which was plenty to choreograph into neat racing scenes. He even enrolled Mario Andretti and the Holman & Moody "Honker" for the movie. There was a Lola T70 for Robert Wagner (RJ) to drive; RJ was Newman's major adversary in the move. Newman's character was named Frank Capua; Wagner's was Luther Erding.

Cinematographer Richard Moore created a number of trick shots for the race cars and the crowd of extras to simulate a real event, over a period of five days. He had one shot where the Panavision camera was half buried so he could get a very low shot of cars rushing into the frame.

He also "under cranked" the camera for some shots meaning when the film was played at normal speed the cars looked to be

Fast & Faster!

about 20% faster than they were actually going! Trick stuff these professionals could do.

Paul and I were closer friends now as he was now driving my car in the film, and at one point he arranged a very minor part for me as a pit crew member. Obviously I was not a Screen Actors Guild member but under the Taft Hartley law I would work the film and be given the SAG membership after. What a privilege and joy that all was. What a great guy Newman was to foster my participation that way! Plus I got to make some personal money!

The pit stop shot would come near the end of the race when the car would need a splash of fuel. I was in a jacket and pants that I had to wear all four days for the film's continuity (they had a staff person whose sole responsibility as far as I could tell was to make sure all the bits were the same from shot to shot.

As the car finished refueling my job was to shout "GO!" to Newman. In the rules of movie making that was considered a "speaking role" which ensured the SAG membership to come. In one take Paul turned around and looking straight into the camera, said, "What! Out there!?" That was all Newman, I believe, not scripted....

Under the sunny skies and beautiful spring weather we continued with getting shots of groups of race cars; I was involved in the arrangement of the apparent competition, the "chorography" so to speak.

The amazing thing to me was that five days of intense work comprised maybe three-four minutes of the actual movie! My part was maybe 3 seconds! The result of that? I still receive a $30 residual from time to time 48 years after we finished shooting the Elkhart part!

There were also some wonderful moments off the track; one evening Paul, RJ and I went out to dinner in Sheboygan, Wisconsin at a nice dinner house. As we sat there I was amazed because every eye in the place was fixed on our table! This, though obviously I was not the object of the attention, I found to be a bit intoxicating.

Newman and Wagner were unperturbed, though, until about midway through dinner (no I do not recall what we had to eat!) a lady approached RJ and asked him for an autograph. Wagner was very gracious and polite as he explained that if he started it would never end, he would miss dinner, and he would be inundated. So he declined. The "lady" stalked off muttering about movie star assholes too good for the rest of us or some such idiot rant. Zero empathy there! That gave me a glimpse of a star's life.... not all rings and roses eh?

One event that gave us all a "moment" was when the film crew installed a Panavision camera mount on the McKee so as to get Newman's point of view. A Panavision camera is a large bulky piece of gear and the camera mount precluded the use of rear bodywork. This would have very serious effects on essential downforce, which was why we made the wedge design in the first place – to make the car stick to the road.

Paul had been driving the car with full bodywork and doing a great job, turning steady, reasonable lap times for the movie. But this lack of rear downforce would make a major difference. I told Paul, watch your corner speed, take it really easy until you see what you have for stick in the corners, and for that matter at speed on straights especially under acceleration. Paul nodded and said something like yeah, okay! That worried me!

But all seemed well, as he heard the car go around with the giant camera hanging on above the engine, and as Pail came by the pits, somewhat slower than usual, we thought well, no issues here.

Then as we heard the car in the back of the circuit, about three quarters of the way around the four miles, suddenly the engine noise stopped and there was a loooong silence! This was NOT good. We sweated it out for what seemed like fifteen minutes abut was actually only two or three at most when Paul came chugging up the hill into the pits trailing brush, sandy dirt, and various other detritus collected as the car ran off the road. No downforce no stickum.

Paul was a little embarrassed but not frightened at all as far as I could tell, which I took as a good sign. He would climb back into the car and continue once the brush was cleared away.

I don't think the point of view shots ever made it into the finished film or DVD stuff though it may have been in the dailies, the previews of that days shooting that we saw every night. I just don't recall!

The script of course had Paul win with RJ second wearing Bondurant's helmet in the Lola. Great shots by a master, Richard Moore.

So that was the start to my 1968 season. Tokyo. Fuji. Hollywood! Wow....

I was having one emotional issue around now; going racing without my lovely wife Evey along as part of the team. Or maybe I should say, part of ME. She was so essential to my life that racing without her there was.... well, uncomfortable when

I was not in the car. I was also dealing with residual issues from the Mosport crash; all the years up until then, with a number of could have been fatal crashes, I had come away with no loss of confidence or any concern that I might get killed doing this. But now there was a baby boy with my name and a wife I cherished and the idea of leaving them bereft was a bothersome thing indeed.

As I am writing this I pause, look around my small apartment in Reno Nevada, notice it is still snowing lightly (about 4" on the ground today), wonder at the paucity of racing memorabilia around me (my younger son Charles E. has all of it, I kept nothing except scanned pictures). It stuns me to be 48 years out from racing. And I still miss it, and Evey, every day (Evey and I separated in 1975).

Not feeling sorry for myself, just noting a fact.

At this point my memory of 1968, through July, is just flat missing and I have been unable to find the missing moments on line. The excellent site racingsportscars.com has no record of me until the Elkhart Lake 500 in July. So I will have to start there. What were we doing? No clues anywhere. We were shown as a DNF at Elkhart but I don't even remember being there at all!

Fast & Faster!

Next record is of the Mid-Ohio USRRC race on August 18th. All I know is I loved the Mk. 10 and the Mid-Ohio course but we didn't do well; the record indicates we ran 3rd in qualifying but a wheel bearing went away. Another DNF.

I have no clue who won!

Or no clue about the next race according to the records, the Elkhart Lake Can-Am. We are shown as finishing 7th, not bad considering the field and the fact that the McLarens for example had at least 100 more horsepower from their huge Chevrolet Reynolds Aluminum engines!

But in essence I was losing both confidence as a driver, and trust in the car. My first race weekend my coach had warned me, back in 1958, that I trusted the car too much. He was talking about the way I flung my Jaguar XK140MC around Marlboro's tight 1.6 miles, hanging the thing out everywhere as if I knew what the hell I was doing!

We were scheduled at Bridgehampton next, and showed up as another DNA – did not appear. I recall nothing about that event or why we didn't make it there. Memories from 48 years ago are a real challenge; I will be 80 this year. So no real surprise there; I just wish I had more to share with y'all.

But as they say, it is what it is.

Fast & Faster!

All this is starting to feel anticlimactic as hell. I was probably focused more on family, my little boy Charles, and the new house we had rented, paid for by my small racing equipment business. Who knows!

At the end of September came Edmonton, Alberta, Canada for a Can-Am race. My wife had a family disaster; her father had been killed in a car accident and she headed back to Maryland to be with her family there. I missed her awfully. And was so sorry for her loss; she was devastated, understandably.

Edmonton proved to be one race where we could actually run pretty well. But in the race, some overheating happened. In spite of that we earned a Can-Am point, finishing 6th.

Next was Riverside, where we had problems again and did not finish due to overheating and fuel issues. Then our season ended at Las Vegas, where we were once again a DNF. The car lost something right at the start, half shaft if memory serves. It didn't help that I had partied the night before and Ralph had to come get me up in time to race. Character flaws. I promised to make this book real with warts and all. That was a big-ass wart!

And that was the end of my career, as it turned out. I had gotten more and more reluctant to trust the race car, and found myself wondering, on the straight during the race at Riverside, what would happen if a wheel came off here. That had never happened before and when it did I knew that was it; I would not race again after Vegas.

My back had chronic pain from Mosport (still does, worse than ever), and that was a reminder that this game could leave my son without a father. Not an outcome I wanted for him.

In the end, I had eleven years in what I still consider the greatest sport ever and lived a dream life what with "Winning", Dickie Smothers, all the great divers, the sights and sounds of America, Canada, Europe and Japan.

And so that is the story of "Chargin' Charlie Hayes", the nickname given me by the press along the way.

Cheers!

Epilogue

It seems like yesterday that I left Las Vegas and driving racing cars for the last time. A lot has happened in the ensuing years, some good some awful. The good parts: I managed a Ferrari agency at one point in the seventies and sold a car to "Rolling Stones drummer Billy Preston, and Diana Ross' husband whose name I forget.

Also I took care of Lou Adler's Daytona Ferrari. Lou fathered the Monterey Pop, was Carole King's producer and his Ode Records brought out "Tommy" with The Who and the London Symphony. I was around for the mixing down from 64 tracks to 16 for Vinyl. What a trip that was!

I also had a decent racing equipment business, we were dealers for Hewland gearboxes and Lola cars through Carl Haas. During that time we built two F5000 cars for a race at Ontario motor speedway's road course. Rodger Ward called me to build one for Bobby Unser with motor home sponsorship; the other was our entry for Ron Grable. We did okay given this was both Formula One and Formula 5000. Don't recall exact result though.

Later in life I found myself doing a search for spiritual truth, and at the same time managing marketing for Earl's

Performance, which gave me a little exposure again to the sport I adore. That was cool. Then I did a stint as a sponsorship marketing coach for racers and wrote a book called "Get Sponsored" which was a popular textbook for that game.

Then I took on my spiritual search big time and wrote several books on that topic. All are on Amazon. The most popular one is called "Life After Death", some excerpts from which appear in this book.

Now I find myself somewhat crippled after a really bad fall that damaged my shoulders (no rotator cuff in the left any more) and having had four heart attacks, resulting in chronic heart failure. I have 45% of the pump left. Debilitating! But I can still do a little writing here and on Facebook (facebook.com/charliehayesnow.)

So that is a life of a racer! Hope you enjoyed the book. Comments are welcome, on Facebook and to charliehayes36@yahoo.com if you are so moved. And donations for health care are welcome; go to www.theeternalstate.org to offer your support or find my GoFundMe link on Facebook. Thanks!

Warm Regards,

Charlie Hayes

Fast & Faster!

Fast & Faster!

Acknowledgements

I thank my friend on Facebook, Dan Samson, for encouraging to write this book. His enthusiasm and inspiring notes mean a lot!

And thanks also to Mark Zuckerberg and Facebook, which has served to reconnect me to many fellow racers and fans from back in the day.

Great thanks to the late Luigi Chinetti for giving a racer his first real chance. And to the late Carroll Shelby for the same.

Thanks to Carl Haas for being a steadfast friend through all the ups and downs of motor racing.

And of course the greatest thanks to my great one time wife Evey for being a true partner for all those racing years.

Fast & Faster!

Fast & Faster!

Fast & Faster!